The Be·ist

Getting Real in a Secular Age

2

"Hear what the Morning says and believe that."

--Ralph Waldo Emerson

4

The Be-ist

Getting Real in a Secular Age

Bay Emerson Bancroft

THE BE-IST: Getting Real in a Secular Age.

Copyright © 2009 by Margaret E. Bancroft. All rights reserved.

The poem "Euclid Alone Has Looked on Beauty Bare,"
Copyright © 1923, 1951 by Edna St. Vincent Millay and Norma May Ellis, is reprinted by permission of Elizabeth Barnett, Literary Executor, The Millay Society.

Front cover photograph:
Licensed from Fotosearch Stock Photography
All rights reserved. Copyright © Nov. 9, 2008

Typeface
Centaur

ISBN:978-0-692-00000-7

Paris
March 22, 2000

An early morning cab ride to Charles de Gaulle Airport for a flight to Boston. The taxi driver, Dev, a retired engineer for British and French Telecom from the Indian Ocean island Mauritius, fluent in English:
> "Mauritius is beautiful, full of guava and mango and longan forests, white beaches, giant land tortoises. An especially good place because people from many backgrounds—Indian, African, Muslim, Hindu, Christian—coexist easily."

Son and grandson of magistrates from Hyderabad, India.
Former head of the parents' association for schools in Paris' 20th arrondissement. Father of a son and a 16-year-old daughter:
> "She drives a car, knows her way around Paris. But she cannot fry an egg—if I ask her to press my shirt, she will do a poor job and will charge me 50 francs."

Fifty-three, afire with energy and curiosity, Dev can't sit still. So he is trying a new career, taxi driving. His topic of the moment on this cool gray morning: the lack of "force" in his children and the younger generation. He finds inexplicable, given such a huge range of opportunities, their casualness and apparent lack of motivation. He despairs that they lack the impulse **"to prove they exist."** *He repeats the phrase five or six times at least, and once more for good luck as we wheel up to the rain-splashed curb at CDG.*

He leaves us thinking....
How do **we** *prove we exist?*

8

So --

To Dev,
To daughter Kate (another one who gets you thinking),
And of course, to Mr. E.

Contents

Introduction: What is Going On Here?   13

Part I. Go Fresh
Chapter 1   Go Fresh   20
Chapter 2   What is Be-ism?   29
Chapter 3   A Case for Be-ism   35
Chapter 4   Secularity Rising   51
Chapter 5   And Why Not Religion?   58
Chapter 6   Who Leads?   74
Chapter 7   Getting Real: 83
                Be-ism in the Mainstream
Chapter 8   "Dare to Be True"   92

Part II. The Job and the Manual (A 1st Draft)
Chapter 9   The Good Wolf   109
Chapter 10   Learn and Teach: 116
                 Acquire Knowledge and Share It
Chapter 11   Act: To Prove We Exist   125
Chapter 12   Do Good: 133
                 Advance Human Well-being
Chapter 13   Do Better: 167
                 Advance the Well-being of the Planet
Chapter 14   Have Fun and Give Thanks   174

End Notes   203
Bibliography   215
Acknowledgments   219

Introduction

What Is Going On Here?

A prevailing sense of our age is that these are confusing and dangerous times. But we know also that great and unexpected changes can turn the tide in society—that fresh leadership and a surge of positive energy can pull us to a standing position, suddenly awake and alive to new aspirations and reborn possibilities. So would it be useful, as together we begin to shape the course of a new century, to aim for a fresh perspective—a *new way* of thinking in the world? In this era of great transitions, would we do well to step back, slow our heartbeat, gather our wits and the facts, and think freshly about our attitude to existence itself?

Meanwhile, does our preoccupation with everyday life—complex and demanding, fraught with local and global troubles—obscure our view of the *most* profound phenomenon of our age? Are we aware of—do we appreciate—our amazing luck in holding front-row seats at the Truly Greatest Show on Earth: the stunning spectacle of a first-ever full-fledged reality-based enlightenment? As we go about our Mondays and Tuesdays, the world and how it works comes into ever clearer focus. The beacons and lasers of science, technology and discovery beam forward, illuminating shadowy corners, revealing ever more distinctly the deep secrets of life and the universe. Living now, we hold the keys, for the first time, to a monumental new kingdom of mind-boggling evidence about the *actual* nature and processes of existence.

For thousands of years, hundreds of generations, our forbears dreamed and toiled—speculated, studied, experimented, and innovated—in their quest to understand themselves and the cosmos. Modern generations carried forward the mission, building on the earlier discoveries and technology, the range and precision of their achievements escalating dramatically through the 20th century and accelerating into the 21st. And now, thanks to the truly remarkable accomplishments of our own contemporaries, we are decoding at last the old mysteries of existence, from the smallest gene fragment to the distant galaxies of the universe. This revolutionary knowledge has been acquired by us human beings ourselves, exercising our unique and extraordinary powers of mind and body, for the first time (most likely) in the multi-billion-year history of the earth. Are we missing the *truly* greatest story ever told, as it rapidly unfolds in laboratories and universities and the real world around us, because there is no effective pitchman to convey—to impress upon us—its importance and significance; and because our attention is commandeered by other pitchmen and programmed for other channels? Is it time for a new, rigorous reality check on the very phenomenon of existence, and our place in it?

The premise in these pages is that existence itself is extraordinary. And that's "all" there is. There is no agenda. The fact, and the facts, of existence are the main point. We begin to comprehend and accept this premise—it becomes self-evident—once we free ourselves from old thinking. Viewing reality directly, we start to realize that in its entirety and its particulars, it is not only sufficient, but so abundant and complex—so malleable and dynamic and extreme—as to leave us humble and amazed. The *fact* of the atom or the i-Pod, the goldfinch or the galaxy, holds limitless power to bend our mind, inspire our awe, challenge and satisfy and entertain us. Given the enormous scope of the real cosmos, and blessed with one finite life in which to travel and explore its stupendous open roads and seductive winding alleys, will we opt instead for the Yellow Brick Road—still holding out for Emerald City, and maybe a date with the Wizard?

We seem bemused, in modern times, by an unsettling sense of hovering and circling—the ever-equivocating "they" (whoever they are) grumbling and doubting we will ever get it right. We sense uneasiness hovering *over* us, too, leaving us sandwiched—trapped and suspended—between reality and "something else." Perhaps it is time now—or soon—to come back to earth: to experience that sensation of *ahhh* as the wheels touch the ground; to stand at last on the *terra firma* of the home planet, our feet on the ground, our head rejoined to our body. As humans we are land animals, but we are vulnerable to so many distractions: so easily our mind, as though independent of our real self, loses or waylays us in the foggy mist of abstraction and speculation and illusion. Can we finally give ourselves permission to descend, and settle on—and settle for—the complex but incomparable rock Earth, on which we live our one real life?

Remember John Ciardi's poem "About Crows":

> "The old crow is getting slow;
> the young crow is not.
> Of what the young crow does not know,
> the old crow knows a lot.
> At knowing things, the old crow is still
> the young crow's master.
> What does the old crow not know?
> How to go faster.
> The young crow flies above, below, and rings
> around the slow old crow.
> What does the fast young crow not know?
> WHERE TO GO."

The young crow, high on flight, frets over the flatness and monotony of the earth below. The old crow sees the forests and plains and cities and seas teeming with unimaginable life, and host to amazing feats of nature, including other crows—and (of only marginal interest to the crow) humankind and all our doings.

Given the astonishing fact of existence—and the premise that there is "no one else out there"—how do we think about our role in the world? How do we, singly and together, play a part, and to what end? Is there – can there be – a purpose which motivates us: a mission which inspires us to forge ahead, experience fully, enjoy deeply, and attain fulfillment from a real life in the real world? A mission which is simple, satisfying, intuitively reasonable, and achievable? Liberated from old thinking, freed up for new thinking, maybe we can focus our attention and energy and hope on discovering or defining such a mission, and then launch into the work of accomplishing it. After thousands of years of diversion—more or less in thrall to an alluring idea of "supernatural" existence and a "Higher" purpose—maybe it is time at last to turn fully to our own human business, to the demanding but rewarding task of proving that *we* exist.

Reality has its own power. It is fresh, immediate, physically present, alive, part of a continuum in time and space, tumultuous yet sometimes infinitely peaceful (as in deep space), always more complex and changing and evolving. We human mortals are part of it – a miniscule fragment, but unique in our ability to understand and conceive our place in the whole, or at least begin to do so. During millennia of relative ignorance about the cosmos, we acquired a habit of awe for the unseen, the unknown, the mysterious, the imaginary—conjuring up theories and mythologies, seductive and compelling stories, to explain what we didn't understand. But at the same time, were we conditioned to *devalue* what is concrete and manifest and real, or to take it perfectly *for granted*, overlooking the enormity of the existence all around us? How is reality commonly described? "Cold," "hard," "mundane," "common," "base" (or even, according to the late theologian Richard Neuhaus, "naked," as in "the naked public square"—barren and soulless, in his view, if you take away the churches).[1] Really? Reflecting upon the discoveries of modern astronomers and astrophysicists about the starry universe, don't we find instead that our old imaginings pale beside the glory, drama, beauty, scope and energy of the *real* galaxies recorded and beamed back to Earth by the Hubble Telescope? As a modern people, can we take up the old motto *Per ardua ad astra*—through work to the stars—but with the actual stars in our sights, and real comet dust in our hands?

In the course of human evolution there is no such thing as an ordinary life or an ordinary time. Like all of humankind before us, we each are living an extraordinary life in an extraordinary time. But here is the difference: we are the *first* human generation to have "how the world works" basically being laid out for us, explained, through cutting-edge advances in science, technology and discovery. In this twenty-first century age, fortified with this huge accumulation of new knowledge, are we "getting real?" Do we comprehend that Existence, in itself, is magnificent and stirring? Will we persist in believing—wanting to believe—that it requires some "other" explanation to give it spirit and meaning? Or is it time now to open the door, let the sun shine in, on the *fact* of our mortality and our life: *face* it, rethink its significance, appreciate it, live it.

If Not Religion, What?

Engagingly notorious contemporary anti-theists such as Richard Dawkins, Sam Harris and Christopher Hitchens publish militant diatribes against religion; but what do they offer instead to fill the "belief" vacuum created by their negativism? Proposed here is a different approach: a case for *hopefulness* – *excitement* even; a positive response to the challenge, "If not religion, what?" The notion itself may strike us as discomfiting or threatening or subversive: the idea of "no religion" or "post religion." But what if it is the other way around? What if superseding religion with a robust set of secular beliefs and practices will constitute a **supraversion**: turning things entirely *right side up* for human society for the first time ever? What if a clear-eyed full embrace of reality will fortify us, more than religion ever did or could, to understand— and thereby to manage and change for the better—the environment (human and otherwise) in which we *actually* exist? What if it will catalyze in us a fresh recognition of, appetite for, and capacity to enjoy the real "best things in life," knowing that we have one life to live, and that the real world is rich with good possibilities for that life? Acceptance of the premise that existence is great and is all there is, plus an inclination to believe that we can identify a worthy purpose for our own existence and can pursue and advance toward that purpose, constitutes a worldview for which a new term is offered here: **Be-ism.** To coin a new name—one more "ism"—for an eminently natural view of existence, may be presumptuous and inadequate and even silly. But that said, could Be-ism step up as the ultimate "ism"? The last (if we should be so lucky)? The one that "says it like it is"?

To Be-ism
So, in anticipation of the inexorable advance of a new reality-based age, the following pages introduce Be-ism, a simple secular philosophy which attempts to close the problematical "reality gap" in our contemporary culture—which suggests a *way to think* about living a good life in an ever-more-enlightened secular world. Be-ism offers a freshly cast premise—one which may hold new promise for the present and the future—in a secular age which already has dawned but which perhaps finds some of us still sleeping in. It asks us simply to face the morning and "hear what it says," and then do our best part to "prove we exist."

※ ※ ※

The Be-ist comes in two parts. Part I, "Go Fresh," is an introduction to and case for Be-ism; Part II, "The Job and the Manual," is a first consideration of how to live a good secular life.

The mission of **The Be-ist** is to launch a new chapter in an old discussion; to serve as the first draft of a contemporary manifesto; to push forward the grass roots movement for a fully secular, sane and civil human society.

PART I

Go Fresh

Chapter 1

Go Fresh

"Why should not we also enjoy an original relation to the universe?"
-- R. W. Emerson
Nature (1837)

Back in 1837, a scant fifty years after the founding of the United States, the radical young American thinker Ralph Waldo Emerson challenged his contemporaries to throw off the shackles of an earlier age and cast their fate with the present and the future – to think freely and think for themselves.[2] Emerson and his peers argued provocatively for a fresh and pragmatic new approach to life, emphasizing the potential of the individual to attain self-fulfillment through a powerful merging of intellect, action and heart. This sea change in thinking was called "the newness."[3] Its advocates succeeded in catalyzing real change in the larger world with their passion for individual liberty and justice, their spirit of inquiry and optimism, their belief in nature, their physical and emotional and intellectual energy, and their faith in human possibility. "Trust thyself," Emerson urged. And then, "Nothing is at last sacred but the integrity of your own mind." The new ideas took hold, changed the way people thought about themselves and the world, and helped shape a new sense of direction for "modern" humanity at that time, a time of frontiers and new settlement, industrialization, and breaking from old European social and economic patterns.

Are we ready now, in our own age, faced with today's array of personal and global concerns, for another "newness," a fresh soul-searching on the subject of belief? As individuals, do we ever worry that—like mindless cells of an expanding self-perpetuating super-organism called "humanity"—we are relinquishing to unwieldy institutions and outmoded concepts our control over the course and the sense of our own lives? The universe, after all, is new every day. It never looks back. We are not fused exclusively and irrevocably to the past or to the status quo, but able to *think* and decide—to some extent, at least—how we will live the current day, and how we will mold our own future.

All along, for thousands of years, we have been "making it up as we go." What makes today so extraordinary is that we are immeasurably more fortified with new knowledge and modern technology. Putting the tools and know-how to use, surely we can come to grips with some of the great problems of our times. They are different from the problems which ignited Emerson and his peers to action: their solutions may depend on our ability to find commonality; strengthen social cohesion; achieve social and economic justice; protect global health; preserve the planet. They may require an enhanced focus on *communality,* rather than individuality. Yet we human beings are social and communal—as well as individual—to the core. Why shouldn't we be able to figure out how to make community work well, and in doing so, advance the mission of civilization for our own generation? Perhaps facing reality with clear eyes and big aspirations is the first step.

"Mind the Gap"

The current expansion of knowledge and understanding of the real world – from the map of the human genome to the dark matter of the vast cosmos – is so comparatively recent and is increasing so rapidly that our minds and our societies have not yet processed or digested this "news" and its import. There is a huge and messy lag—a great gap—between the discovery of knowledge and our success in comprehending it and integrating it into our personal views and our world perspective. Not only have we learned, really for the first time, how existence evolved over billions of years; we also have still with us, live and simultaneously, concrete evidence of nearly the whole continuum (or at least enough to closely approximate it). And not only the living species and minerals and fluids and gases themselves, but their "culture" and their context in many cases. While making discoveries about our own species' evolution, we still share the planet with primates who live in their original habitat and culture; with prehistoric tribes of the Andaman and Nicobar Islands; with African tribal peoples of ancient heritage; with native peoples of Asia (the Mongols) and North America (the Inuit) and Central America (the Maya); with the Maori and other indigenous groups of New Zealand and Australia.

In these old communities our origins co-exist with us, yet we perceive that we have advanced far beyond them in material ways, so our own lives and culture are radically different from theirs. In the grand scheme of human society, how do we manage well this hugely complex co-existence? How do we keep alive—and incorporate for our own use—the best skills and values of earlier cultures, and continue to accommodate their presence in a fast-changing modern world? To what extent will *modern* cultures and societies be able to adapt to new knowledge and fast-changing conditions, while hanging on to their old mythologies and assumptions?

The lag between the stunning new information advances and technologies, and society's ability to process and incorporate them, has generated what might be called the New Confusion: the ambiguity of an increasing divergence between our actual knowledge, technology and capabilities, and our carryover practices and assumptions and expectations, some of them conceived hundreds or thousands of years ago. The fast-growing disconnect seems to have led to widespread social and personal angst, confusion, loss of "moral compass," restlessness, dissatisfaction and dissolution, especially in advanced societies. It is harder and harder to synchronize how we *think* about life and existence, with our actual *experience* and *knowledge* of life and existence. Our attempt to do so fails to deliver the contentment or satisfaction or "wholeness"—let alone the uplift or inspiration—that we seek. Handed-down beliefs and assumptions get in the way, yet have lost the power of their earlier authenticity. Our elders, unable to keep up with the fast-changing times, have lost their old-time authority. We are on our own.

It is perhaps our greatest contemporary challenge: to see clearly, to think through well, the conflicts between old precepts and new understanding; and then—if the arguments and evidence are persuasive—offer up prior beliefs and practices, and change our view accordingly. This discipline—the serious exercise of "keeping honest"—requires all the intellectual rigor and moral courage we possess. Rather than the courage of *conviction* (by definition pre-held), it requires the skill and determination to decipher and face the *implications of the latest knowledge*. It takes place in the demanding realm of *choice*. We can choose to go with reality and evidence, or not. We can choose to embrace metaphysics or other "received" ideology—*decide* to hold on to credulity—or not. The task of sorting out knowledge and arriving at a decision is for each of us to tackle alone.

Most likely—and regardless of whether we realize it—the explosion of new knowledge about the real processes of the universe already has changed human culture and its prospects fundamentally. The old structure is shifting and cracking: winds of change are blowing. For now, a majority of humankind still pays homage to—believes in—a metaphysical power. Yet already, rational, empirically derived, fact-based explanations have supplanted much of the traditional religious mythology about how existence "works." The foundations of religious culture are being eroded inexorably by this flood of knowledge, flowing from genetics and biochemistry and neuroscience; from particle physics and astrophysics; from sociology, economics, anthropology and psychology; from the myriad other fast-moving streams of human inquiry, research, experiment and analysis. At the same time, the rate of acquisition of knowledge is growing rapidly, fueled by extraordinarily powerful and specialized new technology. Won't the same new technology—especially communications technology—lead almost inevitably to *global* dissemination of new knowledge? The more we learn, the faster we seem to be reeling in the unknown—the closer it seems to being within reach.

As new information floods into the culture, doubt and skepticism about the role of *metaphysical* forces grows and spreads accordingly. For conscientious students of the latest science, even "doubt" and "skepticism" express inadequately the erosion of their old religious beliefs. Meanwhile, over the span of many centuries, the church (or mosque, or temple) has evolved into a mainstream cultural force, wielding wide political, social and economic power under the mantle of its spiritual authority. So, in an otherwise sophisticated and pragmatic modern society, an *exception* is made: we raise the flag of religion above the banner of science, holding fast to a "belief in belief"—and to the assumption that our "belief" makes us virtuous.

While religions, and ideologies such as communism, continue to form the "belief" underpinnings of many contemporary peoples, recent global demographic trends show us moving nonetheless toward an increasingly secular and non-dogmatic world society. What eventually will take the place of the old belief systems, which apparently addressed and fulfilled a need in human society throughout long history? What will fill the vacuum, as religion recedes? Are we approaching a fundamental paradigm shift (excuse the term), and if so, what will it look like? What would we *want* it to look like?

"Wisdom" of the Ages?

What about the relevance of old philosophies, as well as religions, to a fresh view of existence? Ancient and modern theories of the universe and existence are rich and tantalizing fare for any curious mind. In recent years, philosophy as a subject has caught the attention of a whole new generation of American college students, "drawing modern-day lessons from age-old discipline as they try to make sense of their world, from the morality of the war in Iraq to the latest political scandal." In 2008, *The New York Times* reports that Rutgers University, home to a top philosophy department, just graduated one hundred philosophy majors, up from fifty in 2002. City University of New York had 322, up 51 percent since 2002. Texas A&M and the University of Pittsburgh boasted twice as many as they had in the 1990s. As the field evolves to include cognitive science and many other disciplines, its appeal and relevance increases. Today's students find that philosophy, with its emphasis on the big questions and alternative points of view, "provide[s] good training for looking at larger societal questions, like globalization and technology."[4] The philosophy majors often go on to become doctors, lawyers, or even investment bankers or commodities traders.

But to plunge into the classical humanities exercise of studying Plato and Kant and Nietzsche—of mastering the *history* of the human endeavor to understand the meaning of life—is too much for most of us. It is hard work. We cannot find the time or the brainpower or the energy for such a gargantuan intellectual task; moreover, we are skeptical of its use in helping us understand our own life and times. How relevant are old theories of existence, unless they hold up in the light of modern knowledge? The great sages were mortals like us. Their fame or notoriety came from thinking innovatively, daringly, in *their* time, acting on the best knowledge available then: a miniscule fact set compared with the one which modern science and technology has made available to us now. How would a contemporary Plato or Nietzsche make sense of humankind and the universe today?[5]

Meanwhile, outside philosophy *per se,* a new generation of broad thinkers has emerged from the hard and bio- sciences (neuroscience, evolutionary biology; astrophysics); the social sciences (political science, economics, sociology, anthropology, psychology); and the many fields of technology (nanotechnology, communications technology, robotics), following in the groundbreaking footsteps of Galileo, Newton, Darwin, Einstein and Crick. The roster of modern pathfinders is far too long to enumerate, but among them we find such leaders as Edward O. Wilson, Jared Diamond, Stephen Jay Gould, Stephen Jobs, Bill Gates, Esther Dyson, Hernando DeSoto and Kevin Kelly. Time may show them and their peers to be the true sages of the post-Darwin secular age.

We can study the classical sages and their modern counterparts. We can do our best, too, to keep up with the latest science and technology—a huge task, but one with big payback in "knowledge" currency. The scholars themselves, and the huge talent pool of their followers in the "media," deliver us the new breakthroughs and discoveries in layman's terms—and even, if we are so fortunate, in clear and lively prose such as the science writing of Natalie Angier (*The Canon: A Whirligig Tour of the Beautiful Basics of Science*); or the hip *New York Times* columns of evolutionary biologist Olivia Judson ("The Wild Side"); or the engaging biographies of Louis Menand (*The Metaphysical Club*) and Robert Richardson (*William James*), bringing alive again the leading American philosophers of the 19th and early 20th century. Altogether, we know the magnitude of our debt to the researchers, scientists, scholars and writers of the world for their evidence-based discoveries, informed speculation, and rich narratives about existence, evolution, ethics, morality, and consciousness. And beyond that, of course, our debt to the other "translators"—the novelists and filmmakers and artists of all stripes who interpret the new knowledge in a thousand creative ways, and deliver it to us, so provocatively, as the latest "entertainment."

But is it not up to us, as well, to do our own speculation and come to our own conclusions about the *implications* –for us and our beliefs—of the modern knowledge explosion? In doing so, how do we think past what has been thought before—"outside the box"? How do we free ourselves from *too much* reference (and knee-jerk deference) to old or new philosophies, to conventional or pop wisdom? How much do we need to know, and be able to recite, about *others'* thinking, in order to come to our own reasonable—or perhaps even inspired—conclusions about our own age?

Originality

If we do brace ourselves to think freshly and originally, will it happen that our own (brilliant) ideas are not new at all, that all this has been said before by [fill in the blank]? Not to be alarmed. Will we shy away from using our own mind, because we might think what has been thought before? (After all, how original is any thought? How can we know? Often we arrive independently at the same explanation of a situation, or solution to a problem.)

Autonomy

Throughout life we guard our own autonomy of thought, or try to. It is the freedom from being told (or even suggested) what to *think* that we insist on instinctively, even from an early age. The authority we rebel against is authority by someone else over our mind, more than over our action. The older we get, the more unequivocally we insist on this freedom. As we mature we seek the views of others—our parents, our friends, our teachers and mentors—in order to develop a sense of the possibilities. We relentlessly seek *facts* from all reliable sources. But we retain what feels like our intrinsic right, to *process* the information ourselves, through our own (absolutely unique) filter, and come to our own conclusions, and modify them as we acquire more information and experience. In any hierarchy or community, we may have to do and behave as we are told or as the community has decided, but we never can be required to *think* as we are told. Our powerful defense is the innate privacy of our thoughts. No one knows them for sure (even when we "divulge" them). In this crucial respect, we retain our autonomy.

We exercise control over *what* we think by getting good information and resisting control by others—a challenging task throughout our life. (Of course children, too inexperienced and dependent to have formed a reliable view of themselves and the world, are highly vulnerable to the influence of others; as they mature, they increasingly assert themselves. Yet even during childhood, the *thoughts* of the child are inviolate: no one else can know absolutely what the child is thinking.) It is mental autonomy that anchors us to a sense of self. Our wholeness of identity—our integrity—hinges on it.

To put the question boldly: Are we sufficiently skeptical of the assumption that "the ages"—with their religions, ideologies and philosophies—have deep secrets and sacred wisdom to impart to us? All there have ever been are *contemporary* human beings and thinkers and searchers, observing and testing and thinking and questioning on the Mondays and Tuesdays of their lives. Do we think they own a special channel to the truth that is no longer available to us? We honor their work, study their methods and discoveries, argue about their ideas. But can we ourselves think originally and freshly for *today*? Can we challenge our (default) habit of looking at today's sunrise through an old lens? What if we crave an authentic sense of the *present* universe – one that will satisfy us now and give us hope for the future? We are accustomed to a role as spectator to the battles among the academics—the theologians and the scientists and the *philosophes*—but what do *we* think?

※ ※ ※

Chapter 2

What is Be-ism?

Be-ism is the ardent acceptance of, belief in, affection for, and desire to know more about *existence itself*. It is actively concerned with all natural phenomena—including manmade societies—and their factual, empirically derived explanations. It is mostly unconcerned with–rejects the notion of—supernatural explanations or agents, and categorizes all "mysteries" as not-yet-explained phenomena. It faces all existence equally—the human species no more significant, *de facto*, than any other—while recognizing our obvious self-interest in the welfare and survival of humanity. Be-ism could be thought of as a short term—a layman's term—for various other polysyllabic philosophical positions: "secular humanism" or "scientific humanism" or "positivism" or "naturalism" (or a new one, "ethical secularism"); but its essence is more active, positive, motivated, grounded and pragmatic. It is a robust, open concept of existence—straightforward, inclusive of all that is real.

In honoring existence and living life, a Be-ist would aspire to be *thoughtful, realistic, ethical, generous, appreciative, curious, active, useful, courageous, modest* and *hopeful*.

To a Be-ist, the unique fusion of qualities which distinguishes each of us from the other— which makes us aware of our own identity, and conveys our identity to others—is the "soul" (if we must think in familiar terms). The soul is the wholeness of a person, the integral-ness, the essence of our alive self. To be whole, we must possess that core sense of self, and must act in synch with it while navigating society and the world. That is the challenge of being fully human in a complex universe. There is no mystical soul to be "saved," or compromised by, or answerable to some imaginary power. It is all up to *us*. There is a well-liked poem associated with the Catholic nun Mother Teresa, who devoted her working life to the poorest slum dwellers of Calcutta:

> People are often unreasonable,
> illogical and self-centered.
> **Forgive them anyway.**
> If you are kind, people may accuse you
> of selfish, ulterior motives.
> **Be kind anyway.**
> If you are successful, you will win
> some false friends and some true enemies.
> **Succeed anyway.**
> If you are honest and frank, people may cheat you.
> **Be honest and frank anyway.**
> What you spend years building,
> someone could destroy overnight.
> **Build anyway.**
> The good you do today,
> people will forget tomorrow.
> **Do good anyway.**
> Give the world the best you have
> and it may never be enough.
> **Give the world the best you have anyway.**
> You see, in the end,
> It is between you and God.
> **It was never between you and them anyway.**[6]

What if the next to last line were to end, instead, with "yourself"? Would the poem then hit home—speak to our heart—because it expresses the innate human tension between our *selfish impulse* and our social, altruistic impulse *"to do the right thing"*? From the perspective of Bei-sm, the "god" of religious believers is in many ways simply a proxy, an unassailable surrogate for ourselves, embodying our own aspirations and sympathies and fears and hopes.

In the Be-ist view, all human beings are born *unique* and *unequal* in their genetic makeup and their circumstances, but with much in common. Regardless of whether we are Maori tribals or European aristocrats or middle-American insurance salesmen, we are fundamentally *alike* in our *humanity*. We generally share a basic premise: "My life and the lives of my loved ones are as important to me as yours are to you."[7] Civilization—evolving from our conscious human compact to improve our lives through material well-being and values such as equality, "fraternity" comradeship), liberty and justice—is a state to which we have come to aspire. In the Be-ist view, an enlightened society strives to provide us—all its members—an optimal opportunity to realize our social and productive potential. At the same time, it demands of us an equivalent effort to be productive and to restrain our antisocial impulses. Civilization: the civil challenge of Be-ism.

What is Be-ism, in sum? A positive working secularity for everyday people.

More than Realism

Be-ism is more appreciative and hopeful than mere "realism." It has a *positive* bent toward reality. It is not neutral with respect to existence, or just resigned ("That's life— grin and bear it"). We do have a positive bent toward existence. We do love life and all the universe. The synthesizing socio-biologist Edward O. Wilson calls the innate affection for life "biophilia," but we might expand the term to "*omni*philia"—an innate affection or attraction for *everything* that exists. Otherwise, why would crowds of ordinary civilians drop what they are doing to spend days up to their shoulders in cold water keeping stranded dolphins afloat along the Florida coast, or lift pilot whales off the beaches of Duxbury, MA, or drive ten hours to Maine to view a solar eclipse, or flock to the slopes of Mt. Helens while the volcanic ash is still falling? We love life and the universe, are endlessly curious about it, and often we will lend a hand if possible. (No one is making us do this.)

Along with a positive view of reality, Be-ism requires positive action: a readiness to work hard and take risks to achieve advances in well-being. It rests on the premise that it is clear thinking and hard work which will eradicate disease, establish fair systems of law and government, and restore health to the environment—that we must rely on ourselves, not on Something Else (or Someone Else) to provide the solutions and do the heavy lifting that leads to a better world. Many of our fellows (perhaps we, as well) experience this challenge as a powerful—sometimes even exhilarating—motivating force in their lives.

Atheism (not...)

Be-ism is not "atheism," for it springs from a belief *in* something (actual existence), rather than a *rejection* of belief in something (the supernatural). In fact, the blunt negativity of the term "atheism" (with its curious pronunciation, *aith'*-i-ism) drastically sabotages the efforts of secular thinkers to convey the powerful positivity of their view. Because they reject religion, they are cast as naysayers, "non-believers;" worse, they are then tagged as lacking in morals and spirituality. The negative branding did not come out of the blue. The world's most famous atheists—political leaders like Hitler, Stalin, Mussolini, and Mao Tse Tung, and philosophers such as Voltaire, his Enlightenment contemporary David Hume, and the cantankerous modern logician Bertrand Russell—inflicted a lasting bad name on atheism because of their socially brutal ideologies and/or their crude and libertine personal *mores*. Rejecting belief in the supernatural, the "bad boys" also rejected—or at least played loose with—morality and ethics. We still face the fallout: society reflexively views the "non-believer" as amoral and non-spiritual. It is a mindset hard to change.

But moral secularists—Be-ists—can take comfort and inspiration from the example of an earlier changemaker, the philosopher Emerson. What was singular about the Concord sage—who fired the imagination and earned the lasting affection and admiration of his fellows and the world—was a rare blend of intellectual and personal traits: the most radical counter-culture ideas (for his time), issuing from the well-schooled mind of one of society's most civil, decent, personally restrained, and kind of men. From an extreme intellect, a refined intelligence. And throughout his career (so rare then and now for a public figure), an honorable and exemplary personal life.

Perhaps Be-ism is the long-overdue antidote to a-theism—and to theism as well. With regard to theism—belief in a god or gods—Be-ism is not just a-theist, but *anti*-theist: it holds that belief in god(s) is in the final analysis detrimental to society, because it hampers the ability of the individual to be self-accountable and accountable to the community. On the other hand, Be-ism is rigorously *ethical*. It is active and questioning, positive. It is perhaps a *default* position for civilized humankind: one we all might hold, had we not been *taught* to be theists, or deists (believing in a Creator), or otherwise to define ourselves in terms of belief in the existence (or not) of supernatural agents. It is a view we might have adopted naturally, informed by the latest knowledge plus our own experience, but unexposed to "received" beliefs.
Be-ism is grounded in, energized by and fulfilled by reality. Borrowing from a phrase we have been hearing, it rests on "the audacity of the truth." It recognizes and celebrates existence itself, and requires that we conduct ourselves well to be worthy of existence. To be—and to do our best at it—is all.

Once we work backward from a realization that there is nothing "else"—that "what you see is what you get"—we start to realign our understanding of existence accordingly. A full-hearted acceptance of existence-as-it-is is profoundly liberating. It parts the clouds of doubt, angst and confusion. It makes one feel "light as a feather." We sense (with apologies to the novelist Milan Kundera) the "incredible lightness of Be-ism." Yet as Be-ism clears and lightens our mind, it also gives us solid ground to stand on, as we consider what we are going to do in our life, and why. Although the future is unknown and unpredictable as the universe unfolds, we need not face proxy struggles with mystical "beings." The world becomes more concrete, with time ahead in which to plan and live and relish our one life.

The Two Premises of Be-ism

Two premises form the basis of Be-ism:

1. *If actual existence—the real world—is all there is, then if we wish to live fully, we will undertake to understand it, experience it, advance (improve) it, and celebrate (enjoy) it.*

2. *Advancing the well-being of our own species and the world is a great and worthy purpose for life.*

The human race always has strived for a better life and a better world. Most of us have a positive impulse toward life: not just to survive but to thrive, and in real time. In the normal course of things, we pour ourselves into the task, bringing to bear our intellectual and emotional resources, social skills, physical prowess.

The progress of humankind depends on the personal force of its individual members, and the communal aspirations of its societies. And sometimes, we must relight the flame. Is it in our communal and individual power, now, to reignite our will (our *good*will) to adopt a simple purpose: to be the best player we can be, adapting ourselves to the realities of the world, while at the same time observing its beauty and absorbing its blows (either of which can bring us to a standstill if we lack resolve)? Do we have sufficient love of existence to make the most of our one lifetime?

* * *

Chapter 3

A Case for Be-ism

The "flash of realization" of Be-ism is simple. It is not that the Emperor has no clothes; it is that there is no Emperor or ever was. The gauze curtain falls away. It was all smoke and mirrors, for thousands of years. However, there are indeed wonderful collections of clothes—and there is indeed a very marvelous empire, of which we are the struggling citizenry. Suddenly we have an entire *real* universe on our doorstep, a universe for real grownups with all their skills and wisdom. What truly can inspire awe in us, is unraveling the mystery of how it got here. What is our true life's work is to understand and play our part in its continuing evolution. The great Massachusetts transportation czar Fred Salvucci used to tell how his Italian forbears came to the USA on the promise that the streets were paved with gold. When they arrived, they found that not only was there no gold, the streets were not paved at all, and guess who was going to pave them? But what was the ultimate triumph here? If we give fair due to the enormous feat of designing and building it, and to the incomparable access it has provided to the vast North American continent, sea to shining sea, for our continuing use and enjoyment, the highway system of the US ranks as a wonder of the modern world. (Of course there is a down side too, as with everything—much hardship and loss in the construction, many accidents on the road, much gasoline burned into the clean air. But as always we must be careful not to take the "up"side for granted. Where are we with our "ribbon of highway"—the "open road"—if there *is* no road?) Do we arrive on the threshold of our productive life having been taught to want the wrong thing: that we should *have* something, rather than *do* something?

    The simple case – the main case – for Be-ism is that it springs from and rests on evidence-based truth (as opposed to *The* Truth): on empirical reality (as opposed to an imagined source or spirit). The cosmos and everything in it does exist. We human mortals (and other living things) do have an active affinity for life and existence. The affinity is a powerful not-to-be-denied force, which energizes our life and influences everything we think and do. It motivates us to enormous effort to learn more about ourselves and the cosmos, and to enhance our experience of life and the cosmos.

As soon as our basic needs for survival are met—physical safety, food, clothing, shelter, companionship—we automatically begin to exert ourselves to attain more knowledge, more skills, more control, better health, more diverse experience, a wider social acquaintance, better food, more stylish clothing, and so on and on. The strong affection for life is simply an innate characteristic of the human condition (and probably of the condition of many other sentient species as well). Although recent science confirms the existence of this biophilia (or omniphilia), it is a fact that—as they say—almost goes without saying. Although it is true that humans or other beings sometimes lose their affinity for life (as demonstrated by suicide and other less extreme indications of giving up on, or assaulting, or condemning existence), and also true that the degree of affinity varies among people and is not constant in a given person, the exceptions cannot negate the overwhelming evidence in favor. To label the affinity for life, and our resolve to improve upon life, Be-ism, is just to give a name to this apparently inborn impetus. Its origins are a subject for psychologists and anthropologists and primatologists and other bio-scientists to investigate and explain more fully, as indeed they are intent on doing; but regardless of what they discover, we know— and the evidence so far shows—that this affinity and this desire for improvement really define our existence as a species.

Spirit and "Spirituality"

Someone we know is admired as a "spiritual" person. But what is "spirit"? What is "spiritual"? According to *Webster's Third New International Dictionary (Unabridged)*, p. 2198:

"spir.it ... [...fr. L *spiritus* spirit, breath; akin to ... L *spirare* to breathe ...] I : the breath of life : the animating or vital principle giving life to physical organisms"
Following the first definition of *spirit* are nine more (summed up):
2. sprites and elves and supernatural or incorporeal beings;
3. usually capitalized, "the active essence of the Deity serving as an invisible and lifegiving or inspiring power in motion" or "one manifestation of the divine nature : one of the persons of the Trinity";
4. "SOUL" or "a disembodied soul existing as an independent entity: the soul departed from the body of a deceased person";
5. "a temper or disposition of mind" or "mental vigor or animation";
6. "the immaterial intelligent or sentient part of a person : the vital principle in man coming as a gift from God and providing one's personality with its inward structure, dynamic drive, and creative response to the demands it encounters in the process of becoming";
7. "the activating or essential principle of something (as an emotion or frame of mind) influencing a person";
8. (archaic) "the emotional source of hostile or angry feeling in a person";
9. (often capitalized) "life or consciousness having an independent type of existence"; and
10. (archaic) "a movement of the air : a breath of wind : BREEZE, WIND."

Then Webster defines "spiritual":
"spir.i.tu.al ... [...fr. L, of breathing, of wind ...] I : of, relating to, or consisting of spirit: of the nature of spirit rather than material : INCORPOREAL --- contrasted with *earthy*."
(This definition also leads to nine more, of which two relate to the religious or divine.)[8] Be-ism incorporates the first definitions of spirit.

Occasionally an "aha" moment lights our mundane or frenetic everyday life: a flash of everything-coming-together when our actual understanding of a situation or a problem converges with a greater sense of "getting it." We experience the rush of a flood of well-being, in our heart and bones as well as our brain, making us feel almost omniscient for a moment, infused with a sensation of power and exultation – the "Eureka!" of the telephone's inventor, on first hearing a live voice over the wires; in football, the thrill of Doug Flutie's spectacular game-saving pass. Momentarily we are high on existence itself. Known words are inadequate to describe the power of the experience: new vocabulary is needed. (Recall the first astronauts struggling to describe their first views of Earth from deep space: the extraordinary sight of "earthrise" across the lunar horizon—the beautiful blue marble against a black void.)

A secular believer feels this awareness of a connection with the cosmos "as much as the next guy" (regardless if the next guy is a Buddhist, a Christian, a Wiccan or a Balinese animist). No religion or ideology *owns* the powerful sensation—which can affect any of us—of oneness with the universe: an uplifting awareness of the dynamic and extraordinary interconnection, the "flow," of existence. As sentient intelligent beings, we know that we *share* existence with everything else, that we are part of the continuum of what has come before and what will come after. The awareness of connection is a powerful, intuitive, warm force which can center us and give us a sense of power, contentment and tranquility. It emanates from us. It is part of us—an animating sense of inclusion, of affection and enthusiasm for life and the universe. It ties us to everything and everyone else. It moves us.

What is truly suffused with spirit is our own experience. Our own life –and the recollection of it—evokes strong feelings of nostalgia, affection, mirth, affinity, whimsy, warmth, tenderness, regret, sorrow, satisfaction. And—the crucial difference from religious "spirit"—we realize this spirit is the expression of *our own* mind and senses and heart. It is our live sense of the congruence between our personal existence and "existence" itself. The state of well-being it engenders—whether calm, elated or ecstatic—is a consequence of our actual circumstances of the moment and how we respond to them. It has nothing to do with a deity, but everything to do with our environment and our self.

Spirit is common, not exotic. It does not set us apart—it unites us. Spirit is indeed "the breath of life." To be spirit-ful or spirit-ed is at least an occasional quality of almost everyone. The "breath of life"—the "animating principle of life"—exists in a Marine Corps drill sergeant or a coal miner, in Ernest Hemingway and Jack Kerouac, in George Soros and George C. Scott—as well as in you or me, or Mother Teresa or the Dalai Lama. To be "spirit-ual" is perhaps to be *more* tuned to, aware of, interested in spirit than usual, in the same sense of "physic-al" or "intellect-ual" or "emotion-al" or "vis-ual" or "music-al". (We *all* possess spirit, physique, intellect, emotion, sight and music sense, and consciously can exercise them if we wish.) In the simplest terms, perhaps we could think of *spirituality* as *full consciousness*.

The strong forces that animate us may be undervalued, in a macho culture, as mere emotions or feelings (by inference soft or "feminine," transitory, not altogether reliable). But in fact these forces—of zest for life, affection for our fellows, love for the earth and waters and sky—are powerful expressions of our humanity. They motivate us to our highest efforts. They give us "proof that we exist." The more informed our spirituality, as a result of learning and experience, the more deeply we feel it. The degree of spiritual awareness—full consciousness—which we attain, ultimately marks, perhaps, the "progress" of human civilization: our knowledge and understanding advances, and thus our well-being, while our spirit strengthens as a result. We join a self-reinforcing upward spiral, if we are able to overcome the obstacles within and without.

Is it worth reconsidering, then, what really constitutes spirit and spirituality? Perhaps, in clearing away the capitals and the mystical aura, we recognize here too an elemental common denominator shared by humankind. Human individuals always will be spiritual—but what requires a special effort, a mobilization of their communal spirit, is for them *together* to become *civilized*.

Prayer

Spirituality brings to mind the practice of prayer. For a secular believer, prayer (if we want to call it that) is not addressed *to* someone or something; rather, it is the private expression of a fervent desire for a good outcome, for good "fortune." Concurrent with the prayer is the understanding that we must act on our own, as best we can, to achieve the outcome we hope for. There is no invisible agent working for or against our wishes, rewarding or punishing us. There is just real life and real forces—and the not insignificant element of *chance*—at work.

Grace

What would be our word—and if there is none, maybe we need one—for what is conveyed by the Spanish term "simpatico"? The word is richer in meaning than the literal translation "sympathy." It suggests a state of *human grace*, if we could be so bold—of being actively in tune with, in synchrony with, our own self and the world: an elevated sense of harmony and well-being which comes from feeling favored (by fortune) in our life, easy in our skin, whole, brimming with affection for existence, even while knowing we are but a fallible speck in the cosmos. We sometimes sense this grace in ourselves or encounter it in someone else. Given the limits of our vocabulary, we may need to coin new words, or look to other languages for existing ones, to describe with justice our newfound sense of secularity and all its dimensions.

Conviction

How can we know for sure what someone else really thinks? We wrestle with the realization that we cannot know the *true* beliefs (if any) of anyone, on questions of metaphysics.
"Where do you go to my lovely
When you're alone in your bed...."? [9]
For that matter, how sincere are our claims about our own beliefs? What are our own real convictions (if any), and do they change over time—or even from minute to minute, with the mood of the moment? To what extent are our "convictions" actually

postures, either trying to convince ourselves or others of our stance, or just "trying on" a position? Are we as sure as we "profess"?[10] And how would our current views change—if at all—if we committed our life to considering carefully *all* the known evidence about existence? Questions without easy answers, but perhaps worth our consideration.

Hedonism

There are rebels in all societies who doubt and battle the prevailing wisdom (religious or otherwise). Often they take a downbeat, contrarian position: they reject the accepted norms without declaring a preferred alternative. Or they embrace a "be here now" philosophy, dedicated to impulsive action and instant gratification of the senses, regardless of consequences. "Love of life" translates into devil-may-care hedonism, untrammeled self-indulgence, *la Dolce Vita*.[11] How do the hedonists fare, in the end? Does a life devoted to gratifying the senses, regardless of others' interests, prove more satisfying than the alternatives? (Janis Joplin, the rebel muse, concluded that "freedom's just another word for nothing left to lose.") Here, the jury is still out. And most of us probably will miss the chance to find out for ourselves....

But unlike hedonism, Be-ism derives from a pragmatic long-term hopefulness: a qualified trust/premise that existence will continue and that it can evolve toward a better existence. Therefore, existence is to be celebrated, studied, enjoyed, marveled at—and the individual and communal *work* of being part of it continues. Good work, alongside good play.

The Slippery Slope of Metaphor

How much do we become captives of our own analogies and metaphors—lose our ability to see a thing directly? Imagination, and the impulse to link one idea to another, can seduce us so easily from looking straight at what we see and recognizing it for itself. Our mind creates and enjoys the image or idea created by the prisms and the mirrors. The landscape becomes "pretty as a picture." The natural world becomes a metaphor for our own interior life. A "brain cloud" keeps us from seeing "the forest for the trees" until "the fog clears" and we "break out of the woods." We begin to see everything *in terms of* something else: either something concrete, and logically associated (the boxer as raging bull); or something abstract, and virtually associated (a film icon as goddess of the screen). Usually the metaphor helps and amuses us—it enriches and enlivens our understanding of reality. Taken to an extreme, though, the associated idea displaces the real thing: the metaphor, in our mind, begins to substitute for the reality. This is the "smoke and mirrors"—the "darkness" of the glass through which we see. We come to *prefer* the analogy. It takes on a life of its own. We walk in to the Fun House, but we don't quite make it out the other side. Our curiosity and liveliness and openness to new ideas and ways of thinking entice us in. But do we exercise the strength and detachment to walk out enhanced—not trapped—by the illusion?

Perhaps it is just this *power of metaphor* which has made religion a virtual reality for so many of us: religion, a great society-transforming example of reality-subversion, which our enthusiastic power of association has made possible. Religion relies on metaphor to explain itself, but the metaphor—like religion itself—is a surrogate for reality, one that is subject to infinite variation and interpretation by us. We hear that "God is love." No. Love is love. Or "God is all nature." No. All nature is all nature. Religion fabricates in our mind an imaginary universe ("heaven") full of real human aesthetics: love, beauty, peace. But in the real world, a secularist would argue, metaphor is no match for reality itself: true human affection, the actual beauty of a real sunrise, the great peace of deep space, or the radiant splendor—from a distance at least—of the Orion Nebula.

Credulity and Delusion

Our ability – even our willingness and desire—to enjoy illusion, or to be deluded, is apparent all the time. As children, we believe in "Hansel and Gretel" and "Cinderella." As adults, we lose ourselves in "Gone With the Wind" or "Casablanca" or "Hamlet." We literally shake ourselves back to reality as we leave the theater or stagger up from the couch. We like magic shows and special effects and "virtual" reality of every sort. At Halloween we (adults as well) enjoy the license to masquerade as Wonder Woman or Spiderman. We succumb without a fight to the phenomenal allure of "reality" TV.

There are the illusions we choose, where we consciously suspend our disbelief. And then there are those we don't, where we fall for deception. Human history is a litany of our (discomfiting, embarrassing, sometimes tragic) vulnerability to being fooled, forced, or sweet-talked by someone in a position of power or prestige into trusting an illusion—into believing that the (naked) emperor is resplendent in ermine and velvet. Even today, as he suppresses and subjugates them, the megalomaniacal North Korean leader Kim Jong Il convinces his impoverished people that they are "the chosen," the "most fortunate," destined to rule the world.

Certainly in dreams and daydreams we experience illusion every day, for better or worse. Then there is our physiological and psychological susceptibility—sometimes addiction—to the psychotropic substances in drugs, alcohol and food which induce "highs" or hallucinations or other states of illusion: a sense of self exaggerated or exalted or transformed, so we "become" temporarily something that in fact we are not. The addictiveness of the illusory state triggered by cocaine, heroin and "meth" inflicts huge damage on society: a personal, social and economic catastrophe. [12]

Also on the dark side of illusion, even harder to understand and to resolve, we face the damage and misery caused by devastating mental disorders which substitute delusion for reality: paranoia, dementia, schizophrenia. The suffering caused by these illnesses is a hard reminder to us of the priceless gift of being *able* to perceive and enjoy the fullness of reality.

We like artifice and illusion for the vicarious thrills and chills, the glamour and romance, the glory and celebrity, the danger and speed, the power and aggression—the kind of experience which is not available to us or "affordable" by us (in terms of cost or risk) in real life. The appeal of fantasy inspires cultural phenomena such as the recent fad for angels: in fiction, in films, in children's stories, at the opera, at Halloween, and certainly omnipresent at Hallmark (at least one to ride on every shoulder). The Cirque du Soleil's 2006 production "Corteo" featured an old clown, dying and embarking on his afterlife in the midst of what could only be described as a "glut" of angels: descending from the tent tops and swinging from the trapezes and ascending back to the heavens trailing clouds of glory and tulle. We like the flight of make-believe, but are we sufficiently self-aware: do we recognize how, and how much, we succumb to the illusion? The sublime *can* lead to the ridiculous. Even short of that, a glut of angels and fairy princesses, Ninja warriors, badass rock stars, and pouting Lolitas begins to suggest a malaise in society: an aversion to facing and appreciating reality; an excessive refuge in fantasy (even perverse fantasy), even for "grownups." Is this what we want for ourselves and our children?

We learn the hard way, through excesses, that an upset in the balance between fantasy and reality can derail us. Reality is a highly demanding domain. If we loosen our grip too much, it is hard to get it back. We develop *habits* of thought and practice, and an "illusion" habit or "escape" habit is hard to break: too many "reality" shows, too many vodka-and-tonics, too much Wii. And it's much easier to lose the balance if reality, for us, is hard. Hence, the special susceptibility of the turbulent young adolescent—or of anyone in the throes of trouble at any age—to drugs and alcohol, or the promised panaceas of religious cults. Especially for the vulnerable, once the reality-illusion balance is off, it is a slippery slope toward harm and danger. Some of us are better equipped than others to face down the dark side of existence without resorting to dangerous "escapes;" but we each can do our best, and try to help each other where possible.

Throughout human life, new brain cells are forming; new neural pathways are connecting and old ones disconnecting.

Because of the remarkable resilience of our brain and neural systems, we have a lifelong ability to upgrade our habits of thought and behavior—but to do so is anything but easy. Surely it makes more sense to make the effort up front: learn to manage our taste for illusion and escape, and rein it in when the downside starts to cancel out the benefit. The balance is the thing— the ability to distinguish between reality and fantasy, and to enjoy both without suffering or causing harm.

Facing the Counter-arguments

"Believers" carry a stock set of first arguments against those who question religion. First, they offer Hitler and Mussolini and Stalin (zealots and ideologues par excellence) as examples of why "godlessness" is evil and dangerous. Then they argue that without religion, we will lose our moral base, and by default will fall inevitably into an abyss of self-indulgent and anti-social behavior.

From the perspective of Be-ism, any ideology, religious or political or otherwise, is anathema to the individual and the community because it vests in *someone else* the authority to control *what you or I think*. It taints and compromises our most precious power: the ability to think for ourselves. In his 2005 commencement address at Stanford University, Apple Computer founder Steven Jobs warned the graduates, "Don't be trapped by dogma – which is living with the results of other people's thinking.... Don't let the noise of others' opinions drown out your own inner voice."

A Be-ist would argue that religion and ideology rule (still) the human realm where the clever and strong manipulate the weak and uneducated. The examples are too many, too egregious and too obvious to name, both over the course of history and at the present moment, but a sample of contemporary analysis (primarily of religion) can be found in Sam Harris' *The End of Faith* and *Letter to a Christian Nation,* Richard Dawkins' *The God Delusion,* Daniel Dennett's *Breaking the Spell,* and Christopher

Hitchens' *God is Not Great,* among many recent dissertations and polemics on the subject.

To the claim that *only religion* prevents humanity from a fall straight and necessarily into moral decay, we might ask for the evidence. With or without religion, human history records continuous and appalling episodes of violence and brutality and subjugation by groups or individuals struggling for power: Egyptian Pharoahs, Christian Crusaders, Mongol hordes, conquistadors, colonialists, Nazis, Stalinists, the Khmer Rouge, Islamic jihadists, Saddam Hussein, the Arab Janjaweed. In the struggles for control and territory, where is the clear distinction between the forces of "religion" and those of "ideology" (or of individual megalomania)? All are characterized by authoritarian leaders who may (or may not) be ego-maniacal zealots. All represent arbitrary and fixed systems of beliefs, and exercise a powerful authority based on those beliefs. The leaders and their organizations use their authority to control their followers, and to persuade or convert or persecute others who do not share their beliefs.

Is there, or has there ever been, an ideology-and-religion-and-autocrat-free society on which to test the hypothesis that, lacking religion or ideology or authoritarianism, a society will descend into brutish behavior? In a world where religions or secular zealots have exercised dominion over people for thousands of years, is there any secular state or community which has organized and conducted itself on purely practical and "ethical" terms? Long ago, maybe Athens and Rome, to some extent, for a while—but with a panoply of "gods" looking on. During the Renaissance and later the Enlightenment, a good start, but with Christian metaphysics prominent in the background. Possibly (and problematically) some short-lived "utopian" communities in the nineteenth and twentieth centuries.

In 1783, the USA was founded as a secular republic, deliberately predicated on the separation of church and state. Of course it was a secular state whose citizens were mostly practicing Christians. Their religion—and eventually other religions as well—inevitably overlapped the public realm, sometimes causing controversy and strife. Even now, "In God We Trust" is stamped on the coins and printed on US currency. American citizens are expected to pledge that they are "one nation, under God" as they salute the flag, and to place their hand on a Christian bible or some other religious text when they take public office. But in her 2006 book *Moral Minority*, the journalist Brooke Allen systematically debunks the popular misconception that religious belief motivated the Founding Fathers in their writing of the Constitution. She shows instead that Washington, Jefferson, Madison and their circle were "skeptical men of the Enlightenment who questioned each and every received idea they had been taught.... The eighteenth century was not an age of faith but an age of science and skepticism, and the American Founding Fathers were in its vanguard."[13] Allen explains further,

"...[The key Founding Fathers] tended to see religious zeal as an irrational, divisive, and even atavistic passion that constituted a threat to human society.... They consistently challenged the religious dogma they heard from the pulpit, both openly and in private, among friends....George Washington rewrote the presidential addresses crafted for him by others to omit all references to Jesus Christ. James Madison gave it as his opinion that 'Religious bondage shackles and debilitates the mind and unfits if for every noble enterprise every expanded project.'"[14]

The rise of the USA to a leadership role in the world usually is attributed closely and particularly to its secular founding principles and values: justice, equality and liberty. In Western Europe, too (especially the northern countries), avowedly secular governments with a strong history of democratic rule govern a largely secular modern populace; likewise, in Japan. Even in Turkey, a new Islamist president governs a politically sophisticated Muslim citizenry under a self-consciously secular constitution. So it seems that a society organized *outside* religion, grounded in secular ethics and principles, can indeed prosper and thrive.

In making a case against secularism, religious arguers assume a darkly negative default: that *as a species* we humans are preset to be greedy, rapacious, hostile, deceitful, uncooperative, gluttonous, adulterous, cowardly and domineering. (And that only fear or love of a metaphysical being—or of a purist ideology—will offset our inherent destructive tendencies.) However, the latest neuro- and behavioral science points to a different conclusion: among the inherent traits which figure dominantly in our *natural* behavior are altruism, empathy, affection and cooperation. New and accumulating evidence shows that these traits impel us *naturally* to advance the well-being of our community as well as ourselves. In his 2006 book *Social Intelligence,* the behavioral psychologist Daniel Goleman cites results from recent research indicating "our brain has been preset for kindness." [15] Arguing that in human nature "the sum total of goodness vastly outweighs that of meanness," he quotes the psychologist Jerome Kagan:

" 'Although humans inherit a biological bias that permits them to feel anger, jealously, selfishness and envy, and to be rude, aggressive or violent, they inherit an even stronger biological base for kindness, compassion, cooperation, love and nurture—especially toward those in need.' This inbuilt ethical sense, he adds, 'is a biological feature of our species.'" [16]

(See Goleman's book, Part II, Chapter 7, for more on the subject of innate "goodness.")

It may be that our default human attitude—all things being somewhat equal—is generally positive, sociable and cooperative. (The great and continuing challenge for us, of course, is to create those elusive "somewhat equal" conditions throughout human society.) While conceding there are real obstacles in the way, Be-ism, contrary to much theism, holds out for the eventual success of the human struggle for well-being—for eventual sanity and grace in our actual earthbound life, in an increasingly free and fact-based and rational society.

Sir Brian Urquhart, distinguished chief of peacekeeping forces (really the founder of modern peacekeeping) for the United Nations from the 1960s to the 1980s, makes a case—curious for a veteran peacekeeper—that "peace" is not the mission of the UN. He argues instead that *struggle* is the natural condition of human societies, and that the goal of the UN is to prevent *struggle* from escalating into *conflict*. If we accept that our struggles (as people, communities, nations) are simply the "givens" of real life, and that our life's work is to attempt to resolve them, using our ingenuity and the many resources at our disposal, perhaps we can face trouble more dispassionately and with a less debilitating sense of grievance . We are not "owed" a better life, but perhaps we can achieve one if we use to the max our natural capacity for good.

* * *

Sandwiched between reality (as we know it) and illusion is the great proving ground of scientific inquiry and scholarly research and general investigation: the gray area, where we do not yet know, but are attempting to discover, the truth of a particular matter; where our advances in knowledge and achievement occur. It is where speculation and hypothesis and counter-argument, data gathering and testing and experiment and calculation, all combine in the driving human quest for verifiable explanations of that-which-is-not-yet-known. Here we actually are "ok." We are on turf which is made more solid by our *recognition* that we do not yet know the answers.

The Challenge of Be-ism

The great challenge of Be-ism, in freeing itself from the culture of religion, is to distinguish between "religion" and the *ethics* of human values and behavior: to separate a *code for living* from *religion*. We must free ourselves to choose good practices, using and cultivating a stronger *civil* sense which builds on our innate inclination to behave well and do good. The challenge is to rise and take charge of our own moral lives, to examine familiar behaviors and practices apart from their baggage of ritual or custom or tradition, in order to understand the *real* motive or justification driving our behavior. Is a given practice *actually* beneficial to the well-being of ourselves and others, or not? Are we vested in the (life-long) struggle to determine what *is* beneficial versus detrimental, and to act accordingly?

If the moral and pragmatic tenets of all religions were screened for common denominators (an exercise attempted by the UN in drawing up the "Universal Declaration of Human Rights" in 1948), achieving a broad consensus on what constitutes helpful versus harmful attitudes and behavior, can we all accept the consequent moral code as *a good in itself?* If so, could our hopefulness be channeled into more achievable aspirations: not to live forever, or meet our loved ones on "the other side;" but instead, to work for better outcomes now for the people and things we care for, in the real world? If we hope and act *beyond ourselves*, perhaps we are more likely to depart content. A good useful enjoyed life is our best legacy.

Be-ism, in expressing and defending its secular stand, must keep its own tenets clear. It must distinguish between secularity and profanity; between helpful and harmful practice; between liberty and license; between self-fulfillment and self-indulgence; between reality and delusion. And we must aim for a wholesome balance between often opposing forces, such as our (very human) love of illusion and fantasy, danger and excitement, and even weirdness; and our conflicting need for order, security, practicality, and sometimes-hard—but also satisfying and sometimes exhilarating—reality.

* * *

So here is Be-ism: a pragmatic and hopeful concept for reality-based people in a newly enlightened and ever-more-secular modern age. If we work hard and well to embrace our secularity and use it to good ends, together we may find a brand new kind of sanity and grace—the sanity of an ever-expanding grasp of real-world knowledge, and the grace of a full and appreciative real life in the beautiful unfolding cosmos.

Chapter 4

Secularity Rising

Kevin Macdonald's stomach-clenching mountaineering film "Touching the Void" (2003) tells the true story of Joe Simpson, a 25-year-old British climber. Simpson, already grievously injured in a fall, tumbles into a deep ice crevasse while descending from a grueling first ascent high in the Peruvian Andes with his climbing partner Simon. Finally *in extremis* after six days of agony trying to crawl out of the crevasse, incapacitated by a badly fractured leg and hypothermia and now facing imminent death, the desperate climber howls his friend's name to the emptiness of the frozen glacier field. In the film, Simpson (who incredibly dragged himself down to the distant base camp, and survived) narrates his story: "I was brought up as a devout Catholic. But I'd long since stopped believing in God. I really believe that when you die you die. … But I wondered if things hit the fan, if under pressure I would [resort to prayer]. [During the seven day ordeal] it never once occurred to me. But I wanted to *be* with somebody when I died." A real life setup, maybe, for "Is there Anyone Else out there?" But Simpson's only craving, in the end, is for a human companion, a buddy, a friend—Simon. How about us? When push comes to shove, what do we really believe? And what, in the end, do we want?

Is secularism a significant force in the world today, and if so, is it growing? On the face of it, it is hard to know. Religious believers and movements express themselves openly, publicly, often passionately (like the Christian and Islamic fundamentalist movements in the United States and the Muslim world in recent times). But crowds usually do not gather in public squares and march in parades and shout into bullhorns to demonstrate a *lack* of belief in religion: to announce that they do *not* believe in life after death or the existence of god. There are exceptions. In Ankara, Turkey in November 2006, Reuters reported, "Thousands of

Turks chanted in defense of secularism ... as they buried veteran leader Bulent Ecevit.... 'Turkey is secular and will remain secular,' chanted members of the crowd, which a police official estimated at 50-80,000.'"[17] (However, several months later Turkey elected its first Islamist Muslim president.) In Europe and the USA there is a Darwin Day Celebration on February 12th each year—formalized by a non-profit organization in 2000, but not exactly a national holiday. The Freedom From Religion Foundation, an American group boasting 11,300 members in 2007, holds an annual convention in Madison, Wisconsin. Yet still, "atheists are viewed far more negatively than any religious group" according to a recent survey by The Pew Forum on Religion and Public Life.[18] We seem to adhere generally to a social and civic etiquette—often imbedded in law—which defers to religion, and which considers affirmations of secularity an unacceptable affront to religion.

By popular consensus, religions enjoy special dispensation and deference, even from those who do not embrace them. There is a general reluctance to offend the "believer." Some day there may emerge a more tolerant and widespread reciprocal etiquette, respecting the worldview of the *secular* believer. Many "progressive" modern nations do declare in their constitution a separation of church and state, and specify certain domains for secularity, such as schools and public spaces, thereby achieving a public realm of "freedom from religion." However, if there is a real *movement* away from religion and towards secularity in the world, it seems to be occurring mostly under the radar—especially so in an overtly religious culture such as the USA. A secular movement, if there is one, would be evident in "degree" as well as "numbers": the individual's religious belief declining in favor of secular belief; and a growing percentage of the populace holding secular views.

Social and political scientists in the 1990s and in the aftermath of 9/11 began to cast doubt on the longstanding theory that secularization of modern societies is inevitable; they argued instead (after seeing the growth of fundamentalism and religiosity in various parts of the world) that the trend is toward "more religion." But in the 2004 study *Sacred and Secular: Religion and Politics Worldwide*, a comprehensive analysis of contemporary religiosity and secularization, political scientists Pippa Norris and Ronald Inglehart conclude that "talk of burying the secularization theory is premature."[19] The World Values Survey (WVS), global research carried out between and 1981 and 2002 in seventy-nine countries with over 85 percent of the world's population (and sponsored or approved by their governments), tracks questions of religion and secularization, as well as many other social and economic indicators of well-being and cultural practices. Inglehart and Norris draw heavily on the rich data base of the WVS and its companion study, the European Values Survey (EVS).[20] They conclude that "the publics of virtually all advanced industrial societies have been moving toward more secular orientation"—and that "modernization...greatly weakens the influence of religious institutions in affluent societies."[21] According to the most recent WVS/EVS survey figures (1999-2001), 48 percent of the combined population of these seventy-nine countries do not believe in "life after death."[22] Using 2006 census data (on the assumption that beliefs did not change greatly in the intervening five years), this translates to over 2.6 billion people who don't believe in an afterlife, of 5.5 billion total in the survey.[23] Asked if they "believe in God," one quarter responded "No."[24] Again using 2006 Census figures, this translates to over 1.3 billion people. Even in the U.S.A., apparently an unusually religious society (especially among the postindustrial countries of Western Europe and Japan), in 2001 over 21 percent of the populace – more than sixty-one million people—claimed not to belong to any religious denomination, and 4.4 percent (twelve and a half million people) did not believe in God.[25]

The WVS survey numbers for China and India, by far the most populous societies on the planet, are of some interest. In 2001, in China (population 1.28 billion), more than 85% of the population were estimated to be either "not religious" or "atheist": 1.1 billion people. However, the survey indicates that 70 percent

(895 million) thought of themselves as spiritual, i.e. thought "about the meaning or purpose of life often or sometimes."[26] For a relatively poor society economically, China's strong secularity is probably a result of its Confucianism (a religion which emphasizes secular-rational values), and its Communist government, which discourages religion—or at least any religion which threatens to disrupt social harmony or challenge state control.[27] In India, a traditional religious society not strongly influenced by Communism, over 20 percent of the population – 209 million people—were estimated to be either "not religious" or "atheist"as of 2001.[28] Even in the USA, Inglehart and Norris detect a "lesser but perceptible trend toward secularization:"

> [T]he trend has been partly masked by massive immigration of people with relatively traditional worldviews (and high fertility rates) from Hispanic countries as well as by relatively high levels of economic inequality; but when one controls for these factors, even within the United States there has been a significant movement toward secularization. [29]

The U.S. General Social Survey (GSS), conducted annually since 1972, showed in 2002 that "weekly church attendance in America hovers around the 25-30 percent region, with a significant fall in church attendance occurring during the last decade."[30] As of 2002, "the proportion saying they never attended church doubled [since 1972] to one-fifth of all Americans."[31] The same survey estimates that the percentage of American secularists, five percent in 1972, climbed steadily during the 1990s to 14 percent in 2002.[32]

Another researcher, Brian Wilson, has found that there may be little correlation between churchgoing and spirituality, "for example if churchgoing in America fulfills a need for social networking within local communities, and if U.S. churches have become more secular in orientation." [33] The WVS similarly finds that in postindustrial societies there is much stronger public support for religious authorities to deal with "the social problems facing our country today" (58 percent) than to deal with "people's spiritual needs" (34 percent).[34] Inglehart and Norris find that globally, in the affluent postindustrial countries, while secularity has increased, most of the societies also show an increasing interest in *spirituality*, in "the meaning and purpose of life."[35] The WVS data also show that in postindustrial societies (but not in agrarian societies), the young are much less religious than the old, and also (significantly), that the modern young do not tend to become more religious as they grow older.[36]

The New York Times reports in October 2006, "Despite their packed megachurches, their political clout and their increasing visibility on the national stage, evangelical Christian leaders are warning one another that their teenagers are abandoning the faith in droves." At a series of leadership meetings in the fall of 2006, the desertion by teenagers was described as "an epidemic." The account quotes Ron Luce, organizer of the meetings and founder of the youth ministry Teen Mania: "I'm looking at the data, and we've become post-Christian America, like post-Christian Europe. We've been working as hard as we know how to work —everyone in youth ministry is working hard—but we're losing."[37]

In February 2008 the Pew Forum on Religion and Public life released the results of a comprehensive US poll, confirming that traditional Protestant churches are in decline. The poll reveals that 25 percent of adults leave the faith of their upbringing; that non-denominational churches are growing; but that one in four adults ages eighteen to twenty-nine claim no religious affiliation.

The data set and conclusions of any poll or survey are suspect to some degree, their reliability being dependant on many factors. Norris and Inglehart observe that "serious difficulties are encountered in obtaining reliable estimates of churchgoing from survey data."[38] They cite other researchers' evidence that "self-reported figures are subject to systematic and consistent exaggeration, due to a social desirability bias concerning churchgoing in American culture."[39] (When the National Election Survey, conducted annually, modified its question sequence to assure the social desirability of *not* attending church, "the proportion reporting that they never attended church jumped from 12% to 33% and has stayed at that level in subsequent surveys."[40])

If there is indeed a general reluctance to "confess to" secularity, or to no religion, the trend to secularity may be greater than the data suggest.

Even if the polls and surveys on religiosity and secularism are not entirely reliable, they do seem to suggest generally that secularism is a significant cultural fact-of-life in the world today, and that overall it is a growing phenomenon, probably unstoppable as the information age and material progress inexorably advance. However, the trend to secularity does *not* seem to signify a decline in people's interest in perennial questions such as "what is the meaning of life?" There seems to be evidence, at least from this broad study, that human *spirituality* does not necessarily equate with *religiosity*. We can have one without the other.

The modern pro and con

Since the Al Qaeda attacks of September 11, 2001, the history of religion has become a subject of newly revived interest and a wealth of energetic scholarship, both in the non-Muslim and the Muslim world: not only the history, but the theology, the rationale for each system of beliefs, and the social and cultural and even environmental consequences of those beliefs. Ardent defenders and passionate critics of every position are weighing in from all parts of thinking society: physical scientists and social scientists, historians, clergy, public policy makers, the media, lay citizens, environmentalists and—via the universal new medium—bloggers of every stripe. Philosophers and scientists and theologians skirmish over big questions and arcane points of doctrine and evidence and reasoning. Their fired-up polemics make best-selling books and hot talk radio, scathing editorials and biting reviews and letters to the editor. The battle waxes sometimes poisonous and personal, a bemusing stream of sarcasm and contempt and smugness issuing from the pens and throats of scientists and other intellectuals—voices of "reason"—and defenders of the various faiths—voices of "charity" and "humility." (Refer, for an example of the verbal war, to a *New*

York Times review by Leon Wieseltier, literary editor of *The New Republic*, of the secularist Daniel Dennett's book, *The End of Faith*. [41] Or, for a rallying of the secularists, see the *New York Times* account of a November 2006 La Jolla conference, "Beyond Belief: Science, Religion, Reason and Survival," sponsored by the Science Network.)[42]

There are many modulated voices too (often drowned out in the shouting): Lewis Wolpert's *Six Impossible Things Before Breakfast: The Evolutionary Origins of Belief*, comes to mind, as reviewed in *The Sunday Times* by John Carey on March 19, 2006. Wolpert addresses the subject of credulity "modestly, without heat," and writes with "neatness and brevity." On National Public Radio, discussion host Tom Ashbrook airs diverse views in an intelligent and civil dialogue on "On Point;" likewise, on Public Radio International, Christopher Lydon moderated lively discussions on the air with "Open Source," and continues to interview his elite "sources" on wide-ranging topics on radioopensource.org. Knowledgeable and well-spoken bystanders weigh in, on editorial pages and in letters to editors and in private discussions, throughout the halls of civil society.

Suddenly it seems crucial to us—crucial even to our survival—to understand and be able to cope with religion-based forces in the world and the power they wield over people and events. This in a curious context in which—for example—practitioners of the most extreme versions of Islam (*furthest removed from a belief in evidence or science or even humanity*) are able to carry out acts of hideous violence using the most cutting-edge secular tools of information and weapons and communications technology.

* * *

The history and evolution of religion is not in itself relevant to Be-ism. However, because religion is the major obstacle in the path to clear-eyed secularism, the following chapter will consider the problem, for Be-ism, of religion and other ideologies.

Chapter 5

And Why Not Religion?

The familiar anti-religion arguments—most recently the polemics of Harris, Hitchens, Dawkins and Dennett—are starting to constitute well-trampled ground, so the reader may want to skip this section. It is included because religion and ideology are the great obstacles to contemporary secularism. To consider how and why that is so, is crucial to the mission of "getting real."

How and how much do *prescribed* beliefs compromise a clear view of reality, and in doing so, steal our integrity, our intellectual autonomy? We need to penetrate the mist: see how religions and ideologies continue to create a fog around reality—scrutinize the machinations of the "wizards," in their many guises, as they perpetuate the illusion of Oz. Are we really aware of—and should we care about—the social, intellectual, economic and spiritual coercion (whether deliberate or not) of their methods and practices? Yes. Any dictated doctrine or set of beliefs which is not subject to question or doubt by its proponents or practitioners *is* fair game. Although the focus here is on religion, it could as well include communism or Maoism or fascism or any other prescribed (by definition, authoritarian) belief system.

How, and how much, *does* religion compromise the ability to see ourselves and the cosmos clearly? Presumably early religions "meant" to offer plausible explanations for events and phenomena before real explanations were known. Regardless of the intent (which itself surely changed as religions proliferated and evolved over several thousand years), the *effects* of religious belief have had a lasting impact on humankind's view of reality. We are products of our own upbringing and culture: how do we achieve enough detachment to take a reliable inventory of our own (or our culture's) thoughts? How do we distinguish between ideas which are "received," and those which are authentic (which we would have arrived at independently, through our own experience and the factual evidence)?

The conflict between a reality-based view of existence and a religious view is irreconcilable. If we truly claim religious belief, the religion *by definition* constrains reality. The positions are contradictory: "God or a metaphysical force rules or orders existence," *versus* "Existence evolved and evolves on its own, without a metaphysical agent." We can't have it both ways. (At least that is the premise of this book.)

Yet even among the elite of contemporary thinkers, some still balk at or wrestle with the contradiction. In May 2008 the prestigious John Templeton Foundation ("Supporting Science – Investing in the Big Questions") asked eight leading thinkers in science and philosophy, "Does science make belief in God obsolete?" The answers ranged from "Of course not" (philosopher Mary Midgley), to "It depends" (Michael Shermer, the skeptic), to "No, but it should" (Christopher Hitchens), to "Yes" (Victor Stenger, the physicist). Stephen Pinker, the cognitive psychologist, responded, "Yes, if by 'science' we mean the entire enterprise of secular reason and knowledge (including history and philosophy), not just people with test tubes and white lab coats." But perhaps Michael Shermer best captured the main point: "Of course, reality does not bend to the psychology of belief. Millions of people believe in astrology, ghosts, angels, ESP, and all manner of paranormal phenomena, but that does not make them real."[43]

Stripped of religion or ideology, our values—principles of thought and conduct—form the foundation of our civilization and the basis of our civil behavior. With religion and ideology out of the equation, we can see more clearly what we are up to. We can observe our culture more critically (in a positive sense). Then we can fine-tune our standards, or reorganize the way we function, in order to improve our civil codes and our institutions. We can plan and act with a clearer head for the personal and the public good.

A lower-case view

An everyday convention which signals deference to religion and ideology is our use of Capitalization. The capital confers Standing on a position or a concept. When we read "God" or "Nature," "Heaven" or "Hell," "Fascism" or "Marxism" or "Communism," they register in our mind as Official: Elevated, Recognized, Important, Absolute. The lower case version—god, nature, heaven, hell, communism – reads as more ordinary, concrete, relative, discussable. Be-ism (although capitalized, for emphasis, in this introductory discussion) really amounts to a lower-case view of life, whereas religion and ideology lean heavily on the capitals. Another such convention is the set point of the common calendar: Time zero = the birth of Christ. We count not from the birth of the planet (too many zeroes), or from the birth of "civilization" (whenever that might have been), or from the birth of our country, but from the (putative) birth day of the Nazarene Jesus Christ. We celebrate a "new millennium" on the appointed day, and count (and think of) the years in terms of *BC* and *AD*. The calendar conditions us to think of time in terms of Christianity.

Through a glass obscurely

The prize-winning biographer Robert Richardson, in a talk marking Ralph Waldo Emerson's bicentennial in 2003, spoke of the "kind of default dualism in much of our thinking....eternity and time, the absolute and the relative, the ideal and the actual, ...spirit and matter...," etc. But he went on to observe,

> "There is something noble-sounding but painfully futile about the first terms of these pairs. The heart sinks when someone starts in about the absolute, the ideal, the eternal, the divine, the universal, the spiritual."[44]

And every skeptic asks a fair question: "Where is the evidence?" Hundreds of millions of religious believers have had thousands of years to produce evidence for the existence of a supernatural entity or force—but so far, nothing. It is a "feeling" they have, an "intuitive knowledge" (usually associated with an ancient passed-down narrative, itself unverifiable or perhaps even conflicting with known evidence). Then they divert the discussion into what a Be-ist might term the "irrational room," demanding evidence that the deity does *not* exist. Meanwhile, the deity (they argue) bestows an unassailable legitimacy on whatever they choose to claim or think (or even do), on however they decide to interpret the handed-down narrative and doctrine: a neatly self-reinforcing view of the universe, and conveniently exempt from the tests of credibility they would require as a matter of course in their "real" life.

The religious believe their religion does not obscure, but rather *reveals* reality (Reality). They rely on historical texts and lore, as well as personal "revelation," to make their case. What has changed over time, though, as it affects the case—changed especially dramatically in the past fifty years—is the preponderance of evidence which explains the actual workings of the real world, from gene science to astrophysics and everything in between. *For those who have been paying attention,* their basic understanding is tipping inexorably from a "mystery"-based to a reality-based explanation of existence. For so many of our old questions about the evolution and nature of life and the universe, the balance between the unknown and the known has shifted to the known. If so much of the "mystery" has been solved, where does that leave the metaphysics?

Modern science and discovery reveal truly mind-boggling and awe-inspiring new information about existence, the import of which we are only beginning to digest. The very fact of each new discovery gives us hope—and good reason to believe—that there is much more to come, of equal importance and complexity and incredibleness. We can marvel at our human ability—in itself still improving—to advance the frontiers of knowledge, and to put the knowledge to beneficial use for ourselves and the world. (And also, of course, to fear its being put to harmful use.) As a community—as a culture—are we welcoming, taking note of, trying to understand, absorbing, using and celebrating all this new information as it emerges? It concerns us. It is *real*. Are we paying attention, or have we been fooled or lulled or sidetracked into missing out on the true "goods" of the world today? To repeat the earlier question, are we "getting" reality?

Actually, more of us *are* paying attention: we *are* starting to get it. Not only in science-oriented publications such as *Scientific American* and *National Geographic* and the newer *Science News* and *Technology Review* and *Discover*, but also in the glossy fashion-and-culture magazines (*Vanity Fair, Esquire*), the literary-cultural monthlies (*The Atlantic, Harpers*), the mainstream news weeklies (*Time, Newsweek*) and the dailies (*The New York Times, The Los Angeles Times, The Chicago Tribune*), science is hot. Writers write about it. Bloggers blog about it. The evening news and PBS specials bring us up to date. Hollywood has noticed and its celebrities are joining the bandwagon to find a cure for AIDS and malaria, to address global warming, to wrestle with the issue of genetically modified foods, to debate and defend stem cell research. Politicians are playing catch-up. Remarkably, we-the-people are discovering, perhaps for the first time in recent history, that "science" produces not only fascinating but *necessary* knowledge, inextricably bound to practically every aspect of our life. In the midst of the science boom, we also find that the distinctions are blurring between science and the humanities and the arts and all aspects of human enterprise and knowledge: that there is a growing convergence and cross-cutting and overlap among domains that used to be considered self-contained. If we are to survive and thrive in the world, isn't it crucial that we understand and support this knowledge-convergence?

In a contemporary scene of widespread political and social upheaval (much of it ignited by turf wars and zealotry in the name of one religion or another), another of our prime social concerns is *security*—the safety and well-being of ourselves, our communities, our nations. In the past, by custom and long tradition we have looked to our church, our religion, our deity, for security and comfort. But in an age where it is the churches themselves which are compromising drastically our civil security, would we not be wise to look to secular practices and institutions to *secure* us from danger and disorder? What *actually* gives us security? Perhaps trust in others (family, friends, community) to help us in times of trouble. Perhaps reliable civil institutions of law and order, and commerce, and environmental protection, and social welfare, and public safety. Perhaps sound up-to-date knowledge about ourselves and the world.

Another reason to question a dedication to religion is the degree to which it seems to *require* dedication. If we must comply with it, "practice" it, repeat its creeds, finance it, submit to it, could it be because it is an *artifice*, a constraint? "Faithfulness" seems to demand constant and repetitive reinforcement, restating, ritual, observance—not to mention a significant outlay of personal funds for the faith. Equally unsettling to a secularist are the religious leaders (even in "liberal" religions) who preach humility but so often convey arrogance: absolute certainty; intolerance of or condescension toward doubt or diverse views. The preachers tell us, to some extent, *what to think*. They may require that we profess faithfulness by reciting texts, participating in rituals, paying tithes and indoctrinating our children. While pronouncing what we can and cannot, should and should not do, they attribute their authority (directly or indirectly) to an obscure unkown-and-unknowable source. (When we discover the preachers themselves perpetrating harm, in flagrant violation of the tenets they teach, we quickly explain the trangressions away: suddenly the perpetrators are "only human.") Preachers encourage arrogance, too, in the congregation: the "believer" is persuaded that he or she is special, chosen, holy, better than others who do not answer to the same authority. (The *non*-chosen are relegated to limbo or eternal torture or some other dire fate. At best, they are condescended to.) Religions' claims of tolerance and ecumenism mask an underlying attitude of superiority and prejudice.

By contrast, a reality-based life, Be-ism, requires nothing of its adherents except *to pay attention*: to digest the flow of information which learning and experience convey to our senses and our mind; and to use what we have learned and acquired to lead a positive productive life. Be-ism relies on skepticism, testing, asking questions, embracing new knowledge and synthesizing it with what we already know. Its authority comes from *us*: ourselves and the greater human community. Its wisdom comes from our historical and current knowledge as to "what works:" what advances personal well-being and the welfare of the human community. A dedication to reality is progressive, dynamic, grounded. It is not proscriptive or prescriptive about how we live: it requires only that we look around, that we are not afraid of the truth, and that we act "as best we can" for ourselves and our greater society, given what we know.

The whole puzzle of religion's obfuscations is too large a subject for this book. But three examples will give the gist of the argument: how "received" doctrine can confuse and mislead us, and—most serious—undermine our natural inclination to appreciate and honor real life and the real world. (Generic Christian examples appear here, but most other religions or belief systems could be used to make an equivalent case.)

The Subversion
Example I. Creation

In reality, all that exists—both matter and energy—exists as a consequence of a complex process of change, affected by environment and hereditary characteristics. We have devoted thousands of years to gathering evidence about earth's—and the universe's—origins, using ever more powerful tools of observation and calculation and analysis, each generation building on the work of its predecessors. We now know conclusively that the home planet is at least several billion years old—in a universe born at least 13.5 billion years ago. We know that human life on earth evolved slowly from simpler life forms, morphing into *homo sapiens* around 200,000 years ago. We test ever more plausible theories about the physical origin and history of the universe. We do not have all the answers—and not answers to the hardest problems, such as first origins of matter and energy—but we have made extraordinary headway. New and continually improving technologies are advancing the rate of our discovery – and the sophistication of the explanations—of ever more new facts and processes. Driving the research is an increasingly broad and talented pool of investigators, players in a global competition for discovery of new knowledge: a global convergence of scientific endeavor. The *ultimate* origin of existence may or may not ever be known by us. But could we argue that it lies so very deep in the past—maybe unaccountably back in time—that it is barely relevant to us or our cosmic view? (Doubtless our curiosity on this primal issue—as around any unsolved mystery—will continue to drive us to seek the answer.)

Closer to home: **in reality**, living things are "created" by various biological reproduction processes. Human beings are generated by the union of one cell from a female and one cell from a male. The cells combine and through a process of multiple divisions and growth, form a new human. As reality-based thinkers, we know and understand the biological fact. We know our own actual origin; likewise, the origin of all other humans and plants and animals.

In religion, it is taught that a deity is the creator of human life and all living beings (and then takes them back to himself at their death). This creates a very different view of "origin" in the mind of a religious believer. How can we reconcile the different accounts? Perhaps by distinguishing between the body (which has a "real" origin) and the "soul" or "spirit" (which comes "from the deity" and is "eternal")? But this apparently simple explanation only exacerbates the confusion and obfuscation: now we, the believers, must consider simultaneously our biological parents *and* our purported religious "father" (the priest or the deity?); we must sort out the actual relationship of our mind and body and "soul" (whatever that is) to each of them—and to the other divinities who may enter the equation. And then, we must understand the relation of the mind and the body and the "soul" to *each other*. Not surprisingly, we, the conscientious believers, are left with an *indeterminate* sense of origin—not really being clear about where we came from or how we got here, or what our responsibilities are toward all those involved, or their obligations to us. Sorting out our origin, and the mutual obligations it might entail, is a perplexing challenge in its own right for a rational thinking person, without adding religious precepts and progenitors to the mix. So— foggy weather on the "origins" front.

The intrusion of religion into reality hits a Be-ist—a secular believer—especially poignantly at baptisms (with "godparents" added to the equation) and weddings and funerals, milestone events in a real person's real life or death. On the very occasion when family and friends and community gather to recognize and celebrate a singular human life—a person known to and loved by them—a religious officiant proceeds to *diminish* the person's authenticity (often in a sanctimonious tone), by giving a *deity* credit for the person's birth, or marriage, or life; and by framing the real life as but a passing moment in a deity-ruled eternity. The "deity" upstages the person—the supposed honoree of the event—and (through "his" agent in the clergy) deflects the attention and honor to "himself." Real life is "put in its place" next to (far below) the imagined realm of glory and perfection of the deity's domain. Once the religious doctrine intrudes, how can we come away with the awareness of having fully attended to— paid attention to—the person being baptized or married or remembered: honoring the child's *real* new existence; expressing joy in the *real* love, hopes for the *real* future, of the couple; understanding, recognizing and paying tribute to the *real* struggles and achievements of the deceased? The "human" part of the ceremony tends to move us. But the religious part, at the very least, distracts us from the subject at hand; if taken to heart, it clouds our understanding of what just happened and wraps it in a confusing (although perhaps comforting) mist of otherness. After the service, the "real" celebration will commence (sometimes to unconcealed sighs of relief) at the reception hall, at home, at the club or the pub.

The occasion is a landmark event in the life (or the passing) of someone we know and like. And there is so much real life to celebrate, to honor, to remember, to laugh about, to grieve over, to hope for.

Example 2. Credit and Blame

In reality, human traits and feelings emanate from inside us. Love, affection, sympathy, empathy, curiosity, anger, jealousy, envy, admiration, scorn, pity, courage, patience, lust, irritability, rage, ebullience, deceit, honesty, doubt, fear, and joy come from within. They are stimulated by a complex tangle of internal and external circumstances. They are mental states which are caused by and modified by emotional, intellectual, physical, social and situational factors. They lead to behavior and actions which are deemed beneficial or detrimental by us and by the community. In reality, we "own" our own traits and behavior and actions, and therefore are answerable for them, to ourselves and the community.

Not only do we own our feelings and behavior, we even possess an innate sense of right and wrong in many situations—an instinctive knowledge of what we should or should not do. Our resident conscience allows us to be at peace with our behavior and thoughts and those of our fellows, or not. The contemporary bio-psychologist Marc Hauser, in his 2006 book *Moral Minds: How Nature Designed our Universal Sense of Right and Wrong*, presents persuasive new evidence for an innate human morality based on honesty, altruism and a reliance on reciprocity.[45]

We also are capable of supreme physical or mental achievement when our well-being or success is at stake, as in the peak performance of a CEO or scholar or athlete in a competition, a soldier in battle, or a mother giving birth.

Each person's history of thoughts and emotions and behavior and words and actions is cumulative, and we are seen by ourselves —and by the community— in the light of this cumulative history. We are not off the hook for anything we do, or fail to do: it all adds up, for better or worse, but with leavening provided by our sympathy and humility, our qualified willingness to forgive or overlook flaws and failings in ourselves and others.

Knowledge that our good qualities (as well as the bad) are innately human can keep us both humble and alert: if these qualities are present in us, they also are present (to a greater or lesser degree) in everyone else. Regardless of our race or culture or class or physical characteristics (let alone our religion), we have no *monopoly* on intelligence or honesty or wit or courage or goodheartedness or wisdom. These qualities exist everywhere in all peoples, without respect to genetic heritage or cultural circumstances (although our environment can enhance or diminish some of them). We have no grounds for a sense of superiority – or inferiority – except our own conduct. Be-ism as a "judge" is universally democratic in that it respects and honors all comers who behave well, and frowns on all who behave badly. And it humbles us with the realization that (contrary to the sometime reassurances of our parents or our friends or our lover) we are not *necessarily* so special after all.

In religion, human traits may be deemed gifts from the deity or the work of the devil, depending on whether they are judged (by the tenets of the religion) as beneficial or detrimental. Taught that our traits come from "outside" (or "below"), how do we keep a sense of ownership of our emotions and inclinations? Without ownership, our sense of responsibility – credit or blame— for feelings and behavior is obfuscated. Not only are we not clearly answerable to ourselves, but we feel at least partially answerable to the outside source, whose identity and predictability is not at all clear. In the midst of the confusion (causing it, actually) are the agents of the religion, trying to explain how it works: detrimental behavior may be exonerated (if requested) by "forgiveness," and beneficial behavior rewarded with a promise of good things in the distant future (in other words, after death). The net result: our sense of self, and answerability to self, is compromised, preventing us from understanding effectively and responding productively to the *real* cause(s) of our emotions, behavior and actions, and leaving us uncertain about what happened. We have a sense of being diminished, and unable to see the world clearly.

If our emotions and proclivities come from Someone Else or Somewhere Else, then where does that leave *us*? We will follow up with some sort of real action, but just "trusting to god" it will all work out for the best. But the price of the confusion and the uncertainly—a high price to pay—may be a profound compromise of our sense of *integrity:* a critical subversion of the sense of wholeness, the ownership of and comfort with our whole self, which is the core of a healthy person's identity. And even more perverse, the "deity" has robbed us of a sense of our *own innate goodness* – of the knowledge that our powerful feelings of love and connection and good will are intrinsic in us, they are *our own*. Grand larceny.

Example 3. Heaven and the Nether Regions

In **reality**, life ends at death for all living things, including human beings. The only "after" life is the physical legacy of our life (what we made or used that still exists) and the memory of us: directly, by our acquaintances; and indirectly, by our reputation and the recorded information about us. So really, *memory* and *the record* are the powerful and marvelous human phenomena which truly perpetuate life after death, keeping alive for us those who have gone before, and storing our own traits and achievements and experiences in the minds and albums and libraries of those whom we leave behind. The memory of the best people we have known fortifies us for our own life: they stay with us; they are a platform under us and a shoulder to lean on and a "virtual" conspirator in a laugh or a thought to share. Of course there is the legacy of our genes, as well, in our children and their descendants—and also the argument that, since matter is neither created nor destroyed, our existence could be considered eternal in both directions.

However, viewed practically, we have a single life with a beginning and an end. If we understand (and necessarily accept) this fact, we become and remain keenly aware that this is our only go-round, that it ends with death, and that our only chance to experience the richness of existence and to make our life a good one is now. Also, that the way we conduct our life is itself the record that will survive, and it will include all our missteps as well as our successes: it is cumulative, from babyhood until we die. Recognizing this to be true, we have a strong incentive to make it the best possible life. That probably is our natural inclination anyway, since the desire to thrive (to achieve optimal well-being) is the innate impulse of Be-ism – is basic to being human.

In religion, the believer is taught to look forward to "eternal life"—a life that continues infinitely after death. Exercising reason, if we are promised that not only will there be an eternal afterlife, but that it will be replete with all good things, we understandably revise our view of our current real life in the context of that assurance. But it is not clear how to do so, since the terms for achieving the perfect afterlife are contingent (although it is not clear exactly *how*) on conduct in the current life. Confusion ensues, and the straightforward incentive to make the very most of real life—to appreciate the extraordinary once-in-a-lifetime opportunity of actually *having* a life—is a casualty of the confusion. The most subversive effect of the eternal-life promise, though, is that it devalues real life and real existence. Suddenly, with heaven for comparison, real life looks messy and shabby and short and full of bad things. It becomes something to be *endured* while waiting for admission to an (imaginary) "perfect" realm. Even the good things of life—the beauty, the love, the excitement, the drama, the triumphs over adversity—are deemed to pale beside their heavenly equivalent, the fictional ideal. We are set up for inevitable disappointment. Our ability to judge the real attributes and value of things is compromised.

Likewise, if taken literally or even symbolically, religion can obscure our view of the unfathomably gorgeous *real* heavens, peopling them (in our mind) with imaginary beings—gods, angels, deceased loved ones, celestial cities—and then proclaiming the whole sky "their" domain. In the same way, religion can taint our true appreciation of the stupendous inner earth—the amazing molten core and mantle and geology of our real planet – polluting it (in our mind) with imaginary devils and ghouls and fantastical extremes of horror. It creates a false yin and yang, *inventing* a deeply disturbing opposition where there is none. It usurps, as its own symbols, the beautiful creations of natural evolution: the lily, the poinsettia, the palm. We are wrong to allow this to happen – to have the real cosmos co-opted in this way, disturbing and compromising our ability to see clearly above and below, and comprehend what *actually* is there. Altogether, religious teaching and indoctrination is fundamentally subversive to the truth of reality. It makes seductive promises which it cannot keep. It may sound good but it is not so: it undermines profoundly our appreciation for the actual substance and scope of life, and consequently, our ability to accept and embrace a finite life in the real world.

Heaven is enough of a damper on reality (as well as a false hope), but then there are purgatory and hell as well, to incite among religious believers the great fear of "messing up" in real life. Messing up is hard in real life—on the perpetrator and the victims—but in real life we often can get past it, partly armed with the understanding that we all make wrong decisions or behave badly at some point, and that our fellows often will forgive transgressions if they can, as a practical matter. And partly armed, also, with the knowledge or reasonable hope that we can offset bad conduct with good conduct. When our own negative impulses cause us to do harm, we have a reasonable chance of understanding and correcting the mistake, and avoiding it the next time, if we can own the problem ourselves (and a better chance, if we have the support of others). And again, a strong incentive to do so, since our cumulative history is what accompanies us, and it is hard to thrive with a bad one.

But once again, given a promise of life after death, of being forgiven sins, and of being able to blame the devil for missteps, a religious person is thrown into confusion as to how to think about

bad behavior and what to do about it. The religious threats and promises are blended with social *mores* and legal strictures.
Obfuscation of the situation once again stymies the striving "believer."

The examples above only begin to suggest the power of religion to compromise our view of reality. They suggest that *the church itself* is the subverting institution in human society. In the guise of "saving us" (from some imaginary dark force), it siphons away our autonomy and intellectual independence. It is a highly subtle force, like a greenhouse gas: in "the air" all around, compromising the welfare of humanity. For those who believe in their faith, the church stands for a higher form of truth. Their conviction itself substitutes for normal requirements for evidence or proof. But for those of us who doubt the existence of a mystic realm, the realization that religion undermines our ability to fathom *reality* will raise an alarm. If we can't "have both," then are we willing to trade the real cosmos, in its extraordinary complexity and vast scope and inestimable beauty, for a comforting but illusive Virtual universe?

"But They *Need* Religion...."

Some will argue, even some secular thinkers, that we "need" religion because so many in the world depend on it. We know that for a multitude of humankind, when everyday life is a struggle against poverty or oppression or terrible loss, reality on its own can seem intolerable. For them, religion offers comfort and hope; and often, as well, subsistence, health services and social support. We cannot know how they would fare without religion and church—or with a substitute such as Be-ism (a love for the real, god-free cosmos), plus a non-sectarian safety net. But would it be presumptuous for you or me to decide *for others* – regardless of their situation in life, or their cultural or economic or personal or social circumstances – that they "need" to believe in something that does not exist? Or is fostering their continuing belief in religion a subtle, paternalistic and perhaps subversive tactic on our part for controlling their fate?

How about a different argument: that *on balance,* even after taking into account the comfort and community which religion confers, its toll on the smooth functioning of global society—on "liberty and justice for all" and fellowship among *all* human beings—is too great a price to pay? Instead, we could work harder to ensure for all people the strength and freedom and knowledge to form their *own* beliefs. We could strive to provide them the means to acquire at least the basic necessities of a decent life. We could focus on giving them easy access to the real lowdown about the universe: a comprehensive modern education.

* * *

So why not religion? Because even in modern times, even among "rational" people of good will, the myths and institutions of religion continue to influence our thinking and our actions. To the extent that they do, they undermine our understanding of ourselves, human society and the world. They cloud our vision, preventing us from seeing that our heart and mind and spirit are wholly integral to our earth-based self. Are we thus trained from childhood as unwitting accomplices in the theft of our own integrity--the ultimate subversion?

Clearing away the fog of religion, recognizing the real universe all around us, we discover that the human mind and heart and soul are not mystical or magical or otherworldly at all: they are as real as a rock or a tree or a beam of sunlight.

Chapter 6

Who Leads?

In the context of Be-ism we could ask, who are the *best* people we know, or know of? Who absolutely tops the list? What are the attributes that distinguish them from the crowd: the special traits or qualities we admire most? In shifting our focus from religious institutions to real world institutions, what sort of leadership do we seek? Depending on our orientation and interests, we gravitate to diverse institutions and leaders in many fields: the physical and social and environmental sciences; the arts and humanities and entertainment; politics and government; technology and industry and agriculture; economics, trade and finance; education and social welfare; medicine, health and athletics. Usually we can find strong, intelligent and effective leaders in any given area: entrepreneurs and business executives; scientists and social scientists; teachers and journalists and coaches; social and medical service providers; designers and builders and technologists; government and law enforcement and military officials; think tank and policy advisers; cultural leaders, innovators and organizers in the many arts.

And then, occasionally, we run across the *exceptional* synthesizers and integrators, those who have the rare ability to conceive and explain "the whole" in a new way, in the context of its diverse parts; or the energy and broad understanding and deep resources to make a major positive impact on their own. Many modern stars come to mind—a different constellation for each of us. For a sample list: the biologists E. O. Wilson, Jared Diamond, Stephen Jay Gould, Stephen Pinker and Elisabet Sahtouris; [46] the internet macro-thinkers Kevin Kelly (formerly of *Wired* Magazine) and Esther Dyson; the journalists Tom Friedman and Malcolm Gladwell; the geopolitical "owls" Mohamed elBaradei (Egyptian-born nuclear negotiator and winner of the 2005 Nobel peace prize), Joseph Nye (former Dean of the Kennedy School of Government at Harvard and author of the term "soft power"), [47] Niall Ferguson and Ashton Carter; the economists Paul Collier (recent author of *The Bottom Billion: Why the Poorest Countries Are Failing and What Can Be Done About It*), Jeffrey Sachs, Jude Wanniski[48] and Hernando DeSoto; [49] the political blogger Andrew Sullivan; the literary and cultural critics Louis Menand, Bernard Henri-Levy, David Brooks, Adam Gopnik and Orlando Patterson; the psychiatrist David Serban-Schreiber; the "baby lab" scientist Elizabeth Spelke;[50] the physicist/cosmologist Brian Greene; the entrepreneurs and human welfare philanthropists Bill Gates, Warren Buffet, and George Soros; the global "social entrepreneurs" Bill Drayton and 2006 Nobel Prize Laureate Muhamad Yunus of the micro-lending Grameen Bank; the philosopher Denis Dutton, publisher of *Arts & Letters Daily* (aldaily.com). [51]

These are the people with extra power of mind, a grasp of the detail and the processes and the trends of our times, and the ability to see the world and its challenges with fresh eyes and imagination and good sense. Together they and their peers comprise an exciting and provocative and wise new class of public intellectuals to whom we can look for knowledge, a sense of direction and inspiration. They talk to—and "speak to" – us. These are the real secular leaders of the community—the brilliant, current, knowledgeable, popular "salesmen" of the Real World. They have the marvelous ability to live locally, but think cosmically. They spread knowledge of the advances and achievements the human community is making in the world, and explain for us the implications of these advances and achievements. They reveal to us the new questions that are being asked, and the new challenges that have been identified. They sort out and synthesize and develop a common vocabulary for the many areas of knowledge which they bring together for each other and for us: in E.O. Wilson's term, they are the emerging masters and mistresses of "consilience." Listening to them, we are buoyed by the knowledge that civilization actually *is* advancing on some fronts all the time (even as it seems to take two steps back on others). We hear "reality rising." Their words, when careful and measured, are an *anti* – polemic. They give us hope, and good reason for optimism, even in the worst of times. They keep us alert. If we keep our attention trained on the best Real World leaders, we ourselves *become* more alive in—and alive to—the world. If we persist in our aspirations and efforts, eventually we achieve standing ourselves as full-fledged players in the game— mature adults making a difference in the real world.

As society's thinkers and innovators collaborate, and cross among disciplines, and cross-reference their diverse knowledge, we become increasingly aware that to some extent, all the "different" fields of knowledge to some extent are *the same thing*—it is all of a piece. It has been all along. But with the evidence now in, and the means of making it available to everyone (as we take it apart and put it back together again), we notice that all is converging. We perceive the information as a whole for the first time, and start to comprehend the extraordinary scope of its wholeness once all the parts are combined. The contemporary philosopher John Searle calls himself a "biological naturalist."[52] The evolutionary biologist Richard Dawkins writes best-selling treatises on theology. The world's foremost expert on *ants,* E. O. Wilson, becomes a celebrated expert on the "macro" scheme of life —the diversity and interdependency of all species—and recreates himself as a leading environmental activist.

The cyber-visionary Kevin Kelly, former executive editor of *Wired* magazine, sees us moving toward a neo-biological era where, as we subjugate technology, the distinction between biology and technology blurs (computer "viruses," neural networks, gene therapy); as the technology becomes more complex and powerful, we start to lose control of the process. Kelly says the "intensely biological nature of the coming culture derives from five influences:

. Despite the increasing technization of our world, organic life— both wild and domesticated—will continue to be the prime infrastructure of human experience on the global scale.
. Machines will become more biological in character.

. Technological networks will make human culture even more ecological and evolutionary.
. Engineered biology and biotechnology will eclipse the importance of mechanical technology.
. Biological ways will be revered as ideal ways.
. Future bionic hybrids will be more confusing, more pervasive, and more powerful….. We should not be surprised that life, having subjugated the bulk of inert matter on Earth, would go on to subjugate technology, and bring it also under its reign of constant evolution, perpetual novelty, and an agenda out of our control. Even without the control we must surrender, a neo-biological technology is far more rewarding than a world of clocks, gears, and predictable simplicity." [53]

The string theorist Brian Greene addresses philosophical questions: "What is reality?" Greene says we may believe that "reality is revealed to us by our experiences," but "modern science tells a very different story."

The overarching lesson that has emerged from scientific inquiry over the last century is that human experience is often a misleading guide to the true nature of reality…. I'm referring to the work of ingenious innovators and tireless researchers – the men and women of science—who have peeled back layer after layer of the cosmic onion, enigma by enigma, and revealed a universe that is at once surprising, unfamiliar, exciting, elegant, and thoroughly unlike what anyone ever expected… By deepening our understanding of the true nature of physical reality, we profoundly reconfigure our sense of ourselves and our experience of the universe."[54]

The distinctions between neuroscience and psychology and sociology fade. "Biological" and "cultural" anthropologists reach an impasse if they refuse to talk to each other, and to the paleontologists too—and the geologists, and the DNA sequencers.

The arts and humanities take up the implications of mathematics and the sciences, even in popular culture. Matt Damon and Ben Affleck launch their film career with "Good Will Hunting," featuring a young and misunderstood math whiz. David

Auburn's *Proof* is a prize-winning Broadway hit in 2001. The same year, *A Beautiful Mind,* the story of the mathematician/economist John Forbes Nash, wins four Academy Awards. At MIT and at Harvard University's Institute for Innovative Computing, science photographer Felice Frankel creates the stunning photographs of orange bacteria or magnetized fluid droplets that jump from the covers of *Scientific American* and *Science*:

"science" transformed by the camera—and the photographer— into brilliant and mesmerizing art, which compels our eye and makes us want to know more about what we are seeing. [55]

In literary criticism and the study of literature, academic disciplines disparaged in recent times as "moribund, aimless, and increasingly irrelevant to ...the 'outside world," literary scholar Jonathan Gottschall argues that "literary criticism could be one of our best tools for understanding the human condition. But first, it needs a radical change: embracing science." Literary studies should "apply science's research methods ... and its insistence on hypothesis and proof;" they should "embrace science's spirit of intellectual optimism." He and likeminded colleagues have found in their own work that "it's possible to use scientific methods to question [and debunk] cherished tenets of modern literary theory, such as the 'beauty myth'" (the theory that in western culture, males maintain dominance by laying exaggerated emphasis on females' appearance).[56] The $1.4 billion Alfred P. Sloan Foundation now gives out around $10 million a year to create bridges between science and the arts: books, films, radio. Vice versa, the same consilience: scientists home in on music and the brain; research advances on the relationship of mental illness to brilliant creativity.

At a more down-home level, the same cross-cutting phenomenon occurs. Take the building trades and the humanities: carpentry and poetry. In Boston, MA, local carpenters from the dense urban neighborhood of Jamaica Plain meet for a beer at a local pub every Thursday night. Two years ago, inspired by published carpenter-poet Mark Turpin's work, they decided to write their own poems each week and discuss them over a brew.

"Thus was born Carpenter Poets of Jamaica Plain. They are 18 men and one woman, and they write of cross-cuts and concrete, aprons and belts, splinters and cuts, posts and beams, plaster and lathe, hammer and nails, the bit and the blade. One penned an elegiac poem called "A Carpenter's Friend," about a beloved dog who accompanied him on each job. They've written about impossible clients and favorite clients. They've written odes to the wood they work with, to the ubiquitous yellow pencil stuck behind their ears."[57]

Taken as a whole, this broad convergence—braiding and meshing all the strands of life together—is the enlightenment, the "newness." It is a stunning feat—this extraordinary consolidation of knowledge and skill: a stupendous accomplishment, achieved only as the reward of many thousands of years of human effort and enterprise. Using forty-six ounces (less than three pounds) of gray matter—our brain—and its associated systems, we are "figuring out" ourselves and our habitat, from the particle level to the galactic, and the beat goes on.

Following decades of increasingly fragmented specialization, leading to a rich but fractured universe of new knowledge, our institutional leaders are beginning to recognize the vital importance of collaboration and consilience. In 1993 Neil Rudenstine, quiet-spoken but visionary president of Harvard University, launched the arduous task of pulling together his many (fractious) departments and graduate schools to consolidate their expertise for the "greater good." The consolidation project, advanced by successor president Lawrence Summers, is being put into play now by president Drew Gilpin Faust, as Harvard embarks on an ambitious science-technology-humanities collaboration on a large new campus in neighboring Allston. At other universities the same sort of synthesis is under way.

Practitioners in the field of "social entrepreneurship" (a term coined by Bill Drayton, founder of the citizen-sector entrepreneurial advocate group Ashoka) play an increasingly significant leadership role at the local level and on the world stage.

They were present in force (in numbers as well as impact) at the 2007 World Economic Forum in Davos, Switzerland: a global gathering of influential leaders from government and industry, but now featuring social- and environmental-welfare "movers and shakers" as well (Muhamad Yunus; Gillian Caldwell, of Witness, which documents human rights abuses; Isaac Durojaiye, who runs a franchise system for public toilets in African slums).[58] Social entrepreneurs work from the principle of collaboration and replication. When they discover "what works" to mitigate a problem in society, they take the idea and run: they recruit "connectors, mavens and salesmen" (in Malcolm Gladwell's *Tipping Point* terminology) to replicate the successful strategy as broadly as possible. David Bornstein achieved long-overdue public recognition for this powerful new citizen-sector force with his much-admired book *How to Change the World: Social Entrepreneurs and the Power of New Ideas* (Oxford University Press, 2004).

In politics too, we hear the call to "get real." Christine Lagarde, France's outspoken finance minister, campaigns for a get-back-to-work revolution to reinvigorate France's economy, declaring that the French should think less to work more. In doing so, she takes heat. "What has escaped my critics," she says with a smile, "is that clearly before action, there must be thinking. But we have been splitting hairs and talking about the sex of angels for long enough. We know the solutions to all our evils. So let's roll up our sleeves."[59]

We also owe advances in our well-being to another kind of leader, not in the category of "thinkers and innovators," but equally powerful in the ability to stir and motivate us. This is the one who by example of great courage and integrity and love—by deed and judgment and passion—shows us how good we can be. We remember Todd Beamer, swinging into action on the hijacked Flight 93 to stop its mission of death and destruction on 9/11/01. "Let's roll." The phrase will always bring a lump to our throat, and make us know we can do better. Our long tumultuous human history reminds us that our best selves can triumph over everyday pettiness when the things that matter the most to us are threatened: life, freedom, justice, honor, and the ones we love so fiercely– our buddies, our lover, our daughters and sons. [60] If put to the test, we may find that these things indeed *are* more precious to us than life itself. (Otherwise, we never will know for sure.)

It is perhaps a paradox that those who do risk their life for us and for our core principles of human freedom and dignity—who place the welfare and integrity of their loved ones and their community above their own life—often are the most indispensable, the "alpha" leaders, the ones we can least afford to lose. In putting their lives on the line for the common good, they prove the greatest love for their fellows and for existence. Their loss is the most grievous. Their example gives us courage to make ourselves worthy of them and also of ourselves. They expand our hearts and minds and our resolve.

Among the papers of a 26-year-old Marine Corps helicopter pilot, killed in action in Vietnam while landing in a hail of ground fire, are two telling pieces: a poem he wrote during his last year in college, and a letter from Vietnam to his younger sister, written a month before he died. The poem:

"His Chosen Instrument"

With an exuberant shout
He thunders straight out
Of town.

He stands on the pegs
And hugs with his legs
The chrome tank.

On the highway he moves
And yells just to prove
He can breathe.

Hands glued to the bars
He streaks grinning past cars
In the wind.

In the country he twists
With strong sensitive wrists
The live wheels.

One with his machine
You can see when he leans
On sharp corners.

Tears stream from his eyes
And some of them come
From the wind.

And an excerpt from the Viet Nam letter:

"My rationale...for being here is ...in the eyes and faces – blue eyed blondhaired faces or black kinky-haired faces – that look up at us in the cockpit when we come into a zone and pull them out of a hot spot. They—these kids—men—18 or 19 may not know why they're here but they're really something. They'll even try to come up in the cockpit and kiss you .. and believe me sometimes it isn't only sweat running down my cheeks. They need me and I can help them..."[61]

Women, as well as men, demonstrate exceptional courage in the defense of justice and the pursuit of equality and the advance of knowledge. They too put their lives on the line and sometimes lose them. They too risk all for us, in war zones and urban danger zones and space flight and AIDS wards. We look to our men and women with "the right stuff." They remind us to aspire to be (as they say in the U.S. Army) "all that we can be."

※ ※ ※

Chapter 7

Getting Real: Be-ism in the Mainstream

A Be-ist world view may speak to us, but it also leaves us with a broad and provocative question. How do we—in a secular modern knowledge-based age—come up with *better* ways of living, of acknowledging and celebrating existence, of "mainstreaming" the concept of Be-ism: ways which are more satisfying, appropriate, and inclusive than our current practice; forms of recognition and celebration which at least attempt to be adequate to the phenomenal, stupendous subject, *reality*. For thousands of years we have extended ourselves—stretched our imagination and skill to extraordinary lengths and heights – to conceive and design and build soaring cathedrals and magnificent temples, elaborate rituals and enormous institutions, to honor the religions and other belief systems of the past. But now science reveals and continues to confirm that the universe evolved by itself. It was *reality* at work all along—for billions of years—forging matter and energy into the cosmos we now inhabit. Can we convert our outmoded reverence for metaphysics into an equivalent appreciation of the *true* processes and history of the universe? (Again, *truly* the greatest story ever told, because it is true.)

Can we re-channel our homage—our appreciation and admiration and allegiance—to the thinkers and researchers and innovators and artists who have succeeded in revealing the *real* truth to us, in beginning to truly explain us to ourselves? Don't we owe this much to the indefatigable scientists and scholars and engineers and technicians who continue to push the frontiers of knowledge, and to produce the technology which accompanies and abets their many missions? (They–the innovators who drive the progress from which we all benefit—are consumed with their work. Maybe it is *our* job to trumpet their achievements.) Like Walt Whitman, should we not be singing a "Song of Ourselves" for our human intelligence and cleverness and tenacity in solving the mysteries of physics and chemistry and electricity and biology and cosmology? How about hymns to the universe itself, simply for existing? Should we not be exulting in our extreme good fortune at being included in real existence—alive in it, and equipped with a brain and senses which empower us to understand it, marvel at and enjoy it?

How can we begin to do justice to the *fact* of reality, and to the pleasure, for us, of our own existence (notwithstanding the obvious truth that it is full of imperfections and causes us pain and suffering too)? As a society whose overall legitimacy rests on the integrity of its individual members, we can start with a commitment to acknowledge new truths and facts and explanations when they are made known. At the same time, we can rise to an obligation to the truth by relinquishing allegiance to disproved mythologies and obsolete institutions. Truth, in the end, wins, and we cannot, in the end, deny it. The historical and present facts and processes of existence are independent of our desires and imaginings. They are what they are, and they will not bend to our wishful thinking that they should be otherwise. In ignoring or denying them, we jeopardize our one opportunity to comprehend and appreciate the matchless beauty and complexity and promise of the *real* creation. The premise of Be-ism is that the *highest* human civilization can only be built on simple truth, not "meta-truth"—on the reality of human nature and the facts about existence.

To be a good Be-ist is easier than being a good deist or theist, because we answer only to ourselves: to our own standard of our "best" self, and our own most conscientious understanding of what is good or bad, helpful or harmful, to ourselves and others and the planet. There is no outside "authority" for whom we perform (or fail to perform), from whom we might hide our actions or thoughts, or to whom we must justify or explain them. On the other hand, it is hard to be a good Be-ist for the same reasons. There is no escaping "the judge:" it is us (or properly, "we"), all the time, along with a jury of our peers.

A Capital "E"?

To pass the concept of Be-ism to a new generation, one person at a time, how do we proceed? Probably as we do now—or wish we did—but more seriously and without "church." We pass on to the children from early childhood our standards and practices for living well in the human community and in harmony with the planet. We try to instill in them the values of honesty, integrity, justice, civility, friendship, consideration for others; the exercise of courage, tenacity and restraint; the habits of curiosity and open-mindedness. [62] Children are serious learners – serious people – from early babyhood. Recent breakthroughs in the neuro- and behavioral sciences demonstrate this fact ever more conclusively. So we start fresh with each new "civilian" who joins our midst, one at a time, and nurture him or her for a best possible life among us.

We observe that religious indoctrination, starting from early childhood, is extraordinarily successful in instilling in the child (and eventually, the adult) a sense of *security* in the church. ("You can take the boy out of the church, but you can't take the church out of the boy.") This sense of security—although founded on myth—is so strong that it frees the "practitioners" even to make fun of, to mock, their own church: the tough nuns, the strictures against sex, and so forth. They can laugh away the *human* dimension of the church because they are bolstered by a strong sense of the presence of an all-loving all-forgiving god (at least all-loving and all-forgiving to members of that particular faith). They are, in effect, inoculated with the fiction of a supreme being, giving them the freedom to just "be themselves."

How do we induce a sense of security and confidence and freedom—but founded on reality instead of myth—in the mind of a secular believer? Perhaps, by teaching the child from an early age of the existence of the universe itself. By nourishing an awe of and love for "Existence" (even if it means resorting to the capital E). By learning (and teaching) ways of appreciating more fully the beauty and complexity of our *actual* surroundings. There are ways. In May 2006, "Eagles" celebrity musician Don Henley, a conservation activist, dedicated "Thoreau's Path on Brister's Hill,"a tract of newly protected land near Walden Pond in Concord, MA. Gathered under a marquee in the pouring rain were the biologist Edward O. Wilson; descendants of Sierra Club founder John Muir, naturalist Rachel Carson, and Lakota musician Chief Luther Standing Bear; and the actress Whoopi Goldberg. But the most stirring presence by far was the children, sixty or seventy nine- and ten-year-olds from nearby New England towns, rain-splashed faces shining. For weeks the young naturalists had been observing and drawing and taking careful notes about what they could find of "nature" in their own yard, and also at Walden Woods. The theme of their project was "Think small, think local, all of nature is in your own back yard." They had produced a stunning array of posters for the dedication: frogs, leaves, butterflies, grasses, trees. The educational mission of the project was well on its way, long before the speeches and applause began.

We are accustomed to the concept of teaching about Nature. Perhaps that is the best we have managed so far, in our attempt to acknowledge the universe. But Nature, in our conventional view, translates as almost too feminine (as in Motherly), too anthropomorphized, too fickle. We owe it to the coming generations to make them more aware of the beauty, the organization, the vast scope of "evolution" so far. We need more gravitas—a more impersonal, grander concept. "Existence" might do better. Even in an affluent educated society, we ourselves still lack (woefully) a full sense of the magnificence of Existence, and of its favorability to *our* life and thriving. We suffer a modern malady which has been named "nature deficit disorder." Alan MacRobert, senior editor at *Sky and Telescope*, says it is a "tragedy of our time:"

> Fewer children (and adults) than a generation ago know the wildnesses around us: the incredible, quiet riches brought forth by tens of millions of years of evolution—the environments that shaped human nature. As a result, people who might have made deep connections with the natural world...instead go

> through their lives spiritually impoverished in subtle but important ways they never quite understand.

He speculates that "cool electronics," the fact that "the neighborhood woods don't advertise," the threat of West Nile and Lyme diseases (and we might add, the distrust of strangers) keep both parents and children indoors. But,

> Winter eliminates the insects, at least. Dress right, and you can laugh at the January cold. And while much of the ecology shuts down in winter, nights can be sparklingly clear. Winter stars are the year's brightest, and the wild universe overhead seems to press especially close. ... Your view of [the Great Orion Nebula] through binoculars is a far cry from the spectacular, wall-size Hubble photographs of its intricate masses swirling with colorful detail. But you are not indoors in a crowded museum looking at a picture. You are out alone in nature, finding the real thing for yourself between bare branches in the wintry dark.[63]

We need to understand and appreciate the entirety of Existence much better than we do now, both for its own sake as a mind-boggling marvel of evolution, and so we don't inadvertently throw a wrench in the works to upset its delicate and extraordinary balance.

A Secular Church?

We may be able to develop new ways of celebrating Existence by looking at what practices and ceremonies work for us now. We know that the religious service for "believers" at church or mosque or synagogue can deliver a spiritual lift, a renewed sense of fellowship, and a re-energized desire and commitment to work for the well-being of the community and the world. The service also gives pleasure through stirring music; incense and flowers; lofty surroundings rich with paintings and sculpture; the glow of candles and stained glass images; the elaborate vestments of the clergy—and even (sometimes) the fetching attire of the worshipers themselves. Usually the institution also provides important social services to the community: hot meals for the hungry; outreach to the sick or disabled or elderly; counseling for personal or social or even economic problems. The religious rituals and outreach services satisfy many of the human as well as religious wants of the congregation and the community.

Possibly a wholly secular congregation could gather as a church, simply to consider and celebrate *reality*. In effect, this would be a church without religion, a church without mysticism. A church honoring and celebrating the best of Existence. A place to consider the known wonders of the real cosmos, and to ponder the unknowns and challenges of life and human society, but in the context of what is actually known, or what seems reasonable and useful to consider, given what already is known. Such a church could foster lively discussion, free from prejudice or arrogance or polemics; inquiry with an open and informed mind; sharing of experience and insights; a rigorous focus on the *positive,* the *hopeful* and the *helpful* in the locale and the world around us. Its members could share a readiness to laugh—a collegial spirit which comes naturally to friends and peers, fortifying each other with ideas and information, friendly battles and humor. A secular church could feature music and art, calla lilies and candlepower, inspired architecture: whatever it takes to revive our spirit and elevate our thoughts, renew our appreciation of "all things bright and beautiful," spur us to work harder to enhance our own life and that of the planet. (And how about the "self presentation" of the congregants? The deep-thinker Emerson, a skeptic in his own church, loved to quote his wife's stylish cousin: "The sense of being perfectly well dressed gives a feeling of inward tranquility which religion is powerless to bestow.")

Perhaps the *forms* of traditional religious holidays could morph into inclusive secular holidays, honoring existence itself: for instance, an end-of-year "yuletide" festival, to celebrate good will, good works, good fortune, good nourishment, beauty, harmony, hope. ("Yule" is from "Jol" –from the old Norse for "wheel." In late December the "wheel" of the year is at its lowest point, ready to rise again for the new year.) Familiar symbols could take on fresh significance: gifts (fortune and affection); cards and flowers (good will); music (harmony and joy); trees and greenery (nature and growth); candles and lights (hope and insight); fasting (cleansing of heart and thought); festive food and drink (nourishment); holiday clothes (beauty and self-celebration). Don't we celebrate all these common human "goods" already—at Christmas, Hanukkah, Divali, Ramadan?

A secular church could be constituted in various ways: perhaps based on interests, or social ties, or geographic proximity, or even "virtual" proximity via the internet. Surely experiments in this sort of fellowship have been and are being tried. The blogosphere no doubt hums with alliances of this sort (and every other sort), and may take the lead in generating at least a "virtual" version of a new type of secular community. It will require experiment and experience to discover what works, if indeed any form of a secular church can gain traction in real life.

Secularity is not a new phenomenon, and its proponents and practitioners have formed many organizations dedicated to their beliefs; but so far, these groups operate mostly at the margins of the culture. In order to generate a mainstream position for secularity, some new kind of organization may be useful, a newly conceived institution and practice for the serious (but maybe not too earnest) consideration of existence, independent of the "church" model. Other forms of secular practice exist already, and have been here all along, either informally (as when friends and colleagues get together and discuss issues of human and environmental well-being); or formally (as in colloquia or conferences sponsored by humanist or academic or civic or cultural groups). When such gatherings occur, do we recognize them for what they are: forums where thoughtful people are considering and defining—for this age—the history and meaning and "purpose" of existence? Regardless of the rallying subject (global warming, community security, Paul Farmer's medical work in rural Haiti, Peruvian folk music), such events, when they "jell," have the power to leave us energized, stimulated, emboldened, hatching new ideas, feeling connected to our fellows and the planet, and liberated (for the moment) from the mundane concerns of everyday life. They raise us up to our "best selves." Recognizing that fact, can we capitalize on it by generating more ways to bring such positive communal events to more of our fellows, more of the time?

It would be easy to dismiss as corny—possibly pointless—the concept of celebrating reality, or "observing" secularity. But simply in fairness, a secular thinker can appreciate that the glass of existence is as half-full as it is half-empty. Could a regular regimen of focusing deliberately on the *full* half begin to revive in us, regularly, the heart and courage and energy to deal with the *empty* half? (For the rest of the time, we too read the papers and blogs, and watch CNN and Fox News and "CSI," and listen to NPR and talk radio, and languish in stalled rush hour traffic.) If we don't go to church (not being religious believers), how do we get together regularly with others, curious like us, to discuss and consider ideas, to find challenge and inspiration, to enjoy a thinking camaraderie? How do we stay connected with our fellows at a high plane, to reap the best benefits of living in a civilized society in an extraordinary world? How do we organize the effort to make human society more civilized, and while doing so, fully enjoy together—as well as take part in—its advance?

Consciously or not, we—at least the enterprising among us—persist in looking for new ways to recognize and appreciate the goods of existence. Our attempts to do better at understanding and living life are a work in progress. We still are trying to find social structures that will produce the best benefits of social interaction, while preserving the autonomy, integrity and privacy of the individuals in the group. We still are learning how and where to draw boundaries: how much privacy (and what kind) is optimal for us, balanced against how much, and what kind of, social bonding and communal activity. We still wrestle with the concept of *trust*: trusting others to guard our legitimate interests, and ourselves serving as trustworthy guardians of others' legitimate interests. (Is it still a bedrock principle of a civilized society: the assumption that family and friends and community and country will be open and truthful with us, and will not act against our well-being, "all things being equal"?)

At the other extreme, does the modern tell-all culture, where we reveal intimate details of our private life and feelings to strangers—in psychotherapy, grief counseling, marriage counseling, 12-step programs, TV shows such as "Oprah" and "Jerry Springer"—lure us into excessive self-exposure? Do we unwittingly—or even knowingly—sell out on self-respect and discretion and privacy?

We have to wonder what "tips" a society into congruence—in its values and its norms and its behavior—with the best knowledge available to it at the time. How long did it take for the "common man" to understand that the world is round, not flat, and what was it that convinced him? If the latest neuroscience shows conclusively that humans' ability to learn new languages peaks at age six and then declines, when will we start teaching children a second language before age six? New cognitive science reveals that the part of the brain which controls judgment is not fully "wired" until our early twenties. How long will it take for society's adults to incorporate this knowledge more effectively into their oversight of teens and young adults, who face a dangerous gap—for us and themselves—between their abilities and urges (e.g. to drive a car, to have sex) and their judgment (to drive safely, to avoid harmful promiscuity)? Who calls the shots in motivating a society to advance, to become more enlightened in its outlook and its practices? What is the most powerful group that is the most highly vested in genuine progress, in achieving the "greatest good for the greatest number"? Who are the "mavens and connectors and salespeople" who actually could change the way society views itself and the world?

So many issues. And these, just a small sample of the full spectrum of unresolved social questions which offer us endless provocation and challenge throughout life. But the questions are of great interest. They deserve energetic attention and study in our continuing quest to learn how best to live among each other at home in the real world.

* * *

Chapter 8

"Dare To Be True"
-- Motto of Milton Academy
Milton, MA

So here is Be-ism: a newly framed view for rigorous realists in a new age, where modern science and thought has redefined and enhanced enormously our understanding of ourselves, the world and the cosmos. The surging advance in knowledge, and the vistas it opens for future discovery, are a huge and inestimably valuable legacy for our generation—a legacy built on the cumulative efforts, imagination and perseverance of tens of generations of our forbears plus a legion of our own contemporaries. We have not yet absorbed its magnitude, its significance, or its implications. But the new facts and their explanations have upset structurally the congruence of our traditional world view. So how do we – each of us – absorb "the news" about the real universe, and fuse it into a reassuring and inspiring *personal* view of existence?

The "Awful Truth"

The past 400 years of modern history have seen extraordinary progress in human knowledge, but they have seen, also, a growing disillusionment in our *attitude* to existence. As the old mythologies and the institutions built around them begin to crumble, we endure a growing unease and insecurity, an erosion of hope and confidence in the future. For a time, the grand experiment of settling the New World, driven by a mission of equality and fraternity and an end to tyranny, rekindled an optimism and enthusiasm for humanity's prospects; but the optimism has dissipated into cynicism and angst. Underlying our unease, perhaps, is a pervasive sense of letdown: the mythology—and the social idealism—which fueled our efforts, and which promised so much (everlasting life, unconditional love, perfect virtue, brotherhood and equality, peace, a state of grace), has not "delivered" as we expected and hoped. Instead we have survived war and enslavement and holocaust, nuclear destruction and airplanes-as-bombs and plagues, hardship and aggression, deprivation and pain and indignity. Worse, much of the damage has been perpetrated by our own species.

By now human society has endured a very long period of cultural deconstruction, where we come to equate "revealing the truth" about old icons and institutions with tearing-them-down (the "truth," by definition, being the exposure of a lie or a stain or a moral failure). "The truth" signifies "the awful truth." Good news is suspect: we demand that it be offset by the downside. (Do we demand that bad news be tempered with the upside?) Devaluing is prized over valuing. We *select for* the negative. We *enjoy* a jaded perspective that the world is all bad and getting worse. Our pessimism is, in effect, a *negative hope* that all will end badly. Hyper-defensive against misfortune, we are unwilling to anticipate or acknowledge *good* fortune. We are smitten with "edginess" for its own sake—in fact, we nurture a *cult* of "edge." We refuse on principle to cut slack for the other guy. (Blast the horn, if he loses a split second when the light turns green).

A hyped-up mission to find fault and destroy idols and second-guess past triumphs stifles our ability to face freshly and fairly and open-mindedly—and with a degree of looseness—the present and the future. But the past is past. The train has left that station. A new landscape unfolds ahead. It is temptingly easy to join a chorus of mockers and naysayers and doomists. But have we really become such a flock of ready-made cynics, a gloomy pessimistic "sheeple"? *New York Times* reporter Shaila Dewan describes the beleaguered residents of New Orleans— abandoning their homes after giving up on the sluggish chaos of "recovery" from the 2005 floods—as victims of "a dissipating sense of possibility."[64] Are the rest of us succumbing too, but without the excuse of a cyclone or an earthquake of our own? (Meanwhile, in

Banda Aceh, the tsunami survivors are picking up the pieces and getting on with their lives....)

The appalling acts of rage and destruction by Islamic jihadists on September 11th, 2001 represented, perhaps, an extreme punctuation mark—a brutal and essentially climactic exclamation point – to our modern descent into societal confusion and conflict (the slope made especially steep and slippery by the growing passion of religious extremists). The "awful truth" took on a new dimension so shocking that it woke us up as a global society. It took us way beyond our familiar angst and into new territory, where perhaps we can look with new eyes, and consider a new start. After a long spell of the doldrums, maybe new winds *are* blowing. Maybe we *can* move beyond our inertia in the face of entrenched social ills and injustice—beyond the fatalistic "boys will be boys," "life is hard and then you die"– and step up to the mark. Perhaps we can start to take the measure of the *full* half of the glass, of our tremendous inventory of human gifts for good, to figure out what we *can* do to make the world a fairer and better place. After a long era of emphasizing the *distinctions* between individuals and societies and "belief" groups, perhaps we can shift the focus to our human *commonality*.

The Upside

In "September Morn," Barbra Streisand croons to Neil Diamond,

"Look how far we've come—
But not so far that we've forgotten
How it was before...."

But *have* we forgotten? How *was* it before? Scrolling back over the long past, do we appreciate how far and fast human civilization *has* come—albeit unevenly—since our ancestors left the cave? On virtually any measure, humanity as a species has flourished and prospered: in numbers, in health, in longevity, in comfort, in physical security, in shelter, in opportunities, in efficiency, in ingenuity, in mobility, in civic and social institutions, in communications, in food production, in material goods, in clothing, in knowledge, in occupations, in amusements, in recreation, in technology, in transportation, in arts, in freedom to mingle with others different from ourselves, in access to all reaches of the planet and beyond.

How about "moral" progress? Read Charles Mann's recent book *1491*, describing the great civilizations of Mesoamerica and Peru in the millennia before Columbus: the *institutional* practices of systematic torture, ritual human sacrifice, mass degradation and enslavement of the losers by the winners. Look at us now: our modern institutions rooted in the notion of democracy, founded on the concepts of equality and liberty and mutual respect, bedrock principles which underlie our national constitutions, our laws and systems of justice, our everyday values. Societies will continue to disagree about how to put the principles into practice—and not all will be "on board" with the principles themselves—but relative to earlier times, as a global society surely we can claim some moral gain.

On a dark day, despairing over how far we still have to go, isn't it is all the more crucial to remember the magnitude of our accomplishments—not only over the course of past centuries, but also in contemporary times? Under assault by a daily onslaught of disturbing news and negative "spin," do we stop, in fairness, to count the recent *gains*: the number of acres of land *preserved* for posterity; the overall *decline* in poverty in the "developing" world; the global *decrease* in child mortality;[65] the *increase* in global life expectancy; the *improved technology* for controlling noxious fuel emissions and recycling old materials; the *speed and scope and efficiency and low cost* of new communications technology; the *vaccines and cures and treatments* for formerly lethal diseases; the *expanded opportunities* for women and girls, and for the disabled; the growth in our culture's *tolerance and appreciation* for racial and ethnic diversity; the *richness* of our increasingly diverse societies (in their people, their cuisine, their music, their dress)? What about the "miracles" we now can perform—the products we can make—with MRI and CAT scans, DNA analysis, silicon chips,

Mylar, spandex, fleece? How about our many other momentous achievements—human feats which were deemed "impossible" earlier in our own lifetime: man walking on the moon; the breakup of the Soviet monolith; political reconciliation in Northern Ireland; the creation of the internet (all those "it can never happen" events)? Can the lively memory of our great successes temper our fatalism, and give us courage and confidence to tackle the personal and global challenges of today?

Another reason for hope, often overlooked (for all its enormity), is the global phenomenon of the Middle Class Rising: the uneven but steady improvement in social and economic well-being in most of the developing nations of the world. At a 2005 forum at the Kennedy School of Government at Harvard University, Professor Merilee Grindle, an authority on Latin American history and policy, identified the rise of the global middle class as our "best hope" for security, justice and equality in the world.[66] Do we realize that global population is projected to peak—perhaps as soon as 2045—and then start to *decline* in this century, the slowdown in growth and its eventual reversal caused by an ongoing global rise in the standard of living? [67]

How about the new generation just coming into play? In 2000, respected "generations" researchers William Strauss and Neil Howe published *Millennials Rising*, a study of the American generation born since 1982; and in 2004 a sequel, *Millennials Go to College*. Strauss and Howe find that, perhaps as a result of being well nurtured by their Boomer-generation parents, the Millennials are *team players*, the *least race-conscious* generation in American history; they are *scholastic achievers* and *hard-working*; they *value unity, respect existing institutions*, are *politically active*; they *honor their parents, play by the rules*, and have an *optimistic* outlook on life. As a group, they have the characteristics of what the authors typify as a Hero generation (like the WWII "Greatest Generation"), rather than a Prophet generation like the Boomers and the Gen-Xers (self-focused seekers).[68] Reinforcing Strauss and Howe's findings, the cultural observer David Brooks describes his students of political theory at Duke University:

"I asked my students to write a paper defining their political philosophy.... When I look back on those papers ..., I'm struck by the universal tone of postboomer pragmatism. .. In general, their writing is calm, optimistic and ironical. Most students...showed an aversion to broad philosophical arguments and valued the readings that were concrete and even wonky. Many wrote that they had moved lately toward the center."[69]

What Millennials may lack in risk-taking and creativity, they compensate for in their concern for community. In 2007, Harvard University boasted nearly 400 student clubs, up from 240 a decade earlier; deans at Boston University and the Massachusetts Institute of Technology report a similar trend.[70] Furthermore, Howe and Strauss find that Millennials are not just an American generation, that "a big slice of the world, outside Islam, Africa and southern Asia, has fallen more or less into the same generational rhythm."[71]

In December 2007, in *Commentary* magazine, Peter Wehner and Yuval Levin discuss the "general feeling of decline" and "social regression" experienced in the USA in the last decades of the 20th century. But then, they say, "a strange thing happened on the way to Gomorrah..." Now, "improvements are visible in the vast majority of social indicators: in some areas, like crime and welfare, the progress has the dimensions of a sea change."[72]

In January 2007 the online journal *Edge* asked ten leading American thinkers from the fields of science, technology, psychology, education and journalism, "What are you optimistic about?" A sample of their responses:

Geoffrey Carr (Science Editor, *The Economist*), on human population growth:

"When I was growing up, the problem at the heart of every environmental problem was human population growth..... Such pessimism, however, failed to take account of the demographic shift [downward] that all populations (so far) have gone as they have enriched themselves, [caused by]the thing that the doomsters feared most after population growth – economic growth.... It flies in the face of common sense that population growth will actually slow down in the face of better resources. But that is what happens, and it might yet save humanity from the fate predicted for it by the Club of Rome."

Chris Anderson (Curator, TED Conference), on the media:
"Certain types of news – for example dramatic disasters and terrorist actions – are massively over-reported, others—such as scientific progress and meaningful statistical surveys of the state of the world – massively under-reported.... Once you realize you're being inadvertently brainwashed to believe things are worse than they are, you can ... with a little courage ... step out into the sunshine. ...Rottweiler Savages Baby is a bigger story than Poverty Percentage Falls even though the latter is a story about better lives for millions.... Meta-level reporting doesn't get much of a look-in. ..[T]he publication last year of a carefully researched Human Security Report received little attention. Despite the fact that it had concluded that the numbers [sic] of armed conflicts in the world had *fallen* 40% in little over a decade. And the number of fatalities per conflict also had fallen... In fact, most meta-level reporting of trends show [sic] a world that is getting better... If that doesn't make us happier, we really have no one to blame except ourselves."

Howard Gardner (Psychologist), on learning disabilities:
"I think of the early detection of learning disabilities or difficulties, coupled with interventions that can ameliorate or even dissipate these difficulties...[using] neural imaging techniques....[T]he more specific the detection of the disorder, the more likely that we can ultimately devise interventions that directly address a particular problem."

Marc D. Hauser (Psychologist and Biologist), on prejudice:
"The good news is that science is uncovering some of the details of [humans'] destructive capacity [to demote the other and raise the self], and may hold the key to an applied solution: if we play our cards correctly, we may see the day when our instinctive prejudice toward *the other* will dissolve, gaining greater respect for differences, expanding our moral circle..."

Stephen Pinker (Psychologist), on violence:
> "..[A]s far as I know, every systematic attempt to document the prevalence of violence over centuries and millennia ... particularly in the West, has shown that the overall trend is downward (though of course with many zigzags).... My optimism lies in the hope that the decline of force over the centuries is a real phenomenon, that is the product of systematic forces that will continue to operate, and that we can identify those forces and perhaps concentrate and bottle them." [73]

On the home front, we are on a huge venture of discovery about each other and the world. Look at the spectrum of existence in our own daily domain – our friends and colleagues and acquaintances; our material possessions; our access to telecommunications and other technologies; our variety of entertainment; our ability to select and indulge in our special enthusiasms (Tuscan wines, Chilean textiles, small-boat sailing, medieval history, Tai C'i, blogging, supporting Tibetan refugees, studying Mandarin). This is no longer "your grandparents'" world. It is a great global smorgasbord laid out in front of us. But it is up to us to show up at the table—to help ourselves from "the full cupboard of life" (borrowing the title of one of Alexander McCall Smith's popular Botswana novels).

What actually are we up to, in the macro sense, as a prolific thinking modern species? We detect, "solve" order in the real world around us—in the relationships among its elements and our relationships to them. Exploiting our knowledge and understanding, we create around us an increasingly complex and orderly and innovative civilization. We press on relentlessly to do more of both—the understanding and "seeing," and the design and construction of our human habitat—pursuing an ever-more-complex undertaking. As we proceed, there are more and more of us (so far), with more "advantages" and skills and resources to continue the project. We try to maintain and repair what we have already made, while advancing the leading edge—shoring up the collapses in our wake, while building new at the frontier. An extreme metaphor for our ongoing civilization process could be the new urban mega-project rising and spreading at the confluence of the White and Blue Nile in Khartoum, Sudan—Africa's largest commercial construction site. *The Economist* reports:

> "Across 1,500 acres, at a place called Alsunut, Sudanese and Chinese workmen are working in shifts around the clock to build a new Dubai: a vast complex of gleaming offices, duplexes and golf courses that will turn Khartoum, it is hoped, into the commercial and financial hub of Islamist east Africa....
>
> But this, of course, is not the whole story. Behind the fast-rising glittering towers lies a region that has been ignored: Sudan's south... This [oil rich] region, which holds the key to the development of Sudan, also holds the key to its peace in future; not only in the south, but also in the war-ravaged western region of Darfur."[74]

The latest technology and the gleaming highrises emerge at the forefront; but in their distant wake in the pastoral villages of Darfur, the rural people endure tribal mayhem, both primitive and high-tech (marauding Janjaweed on camels and horseback, helicopter gunships from above). We can rate the "new" Khartoum a gleaming success or a travesty, a triumph or a tragedy, in its implications about what motivates us, how we harness resources, how we care about each other and our lives and the planet. But are we served by a rush to judgment in either direction? Can we aim for a more incisive consideration of what actually is happening in Sudan, and why?

It is a long time since we as a society have held a confident and optimistic worldview, and we are conditioned to resist a hopeful outlook. But if we claim to believe in fairness and open minds, perhaps we can try for more balance. In doing so, we may start to appreciate more clearly the extraordinary upside of our lives and of existence. As a species we still have an eye for beauty, an ear for harmony, a feeling for pleasure and soundness, a thirst for knowledge, and a taste for success. We can *choose* between a passive pessimism and an active optimism—or at least an invigorating "sense of the possibilities." Acting for ourselves, we *can* restore positive thinking and forward motion to the common human project of civil-ization.

Too Soon?

Is the concept of an entirely secular existence—and an entirely reality-based philosophy—still too new for a culture which is so invested in and so wedded to a core belief in something "other"? Is the intractability of our old convictions – the strength of our belief in "belief"—still too strong to allow us to accept and embrace fully both the astounding realities and the finite limits of the actual world? Are we too afraid of "losing" our old faith, even when we know it is based on myth? Are we unable to digest the fact that all today's people were born in today's world – that they have no more access to historic or special knowledge or wisdom than you or I? Are we so accustomed to "they" (whoever they are) being in control of our institutions and our ideas that we cannot adjust to the fact that it is just *us*? Probably so, for most people, for the moment.

Yet for those of us who are on the fence, it may be useful to track the evolution in thinking of the some of the *best* minds of our time: the "thought leaders," those who seem able to process the full spectrum of current knowledge (in other words, who possess *more knowledge* than the rest of us), and then can distill the whole into a synthesized cosmic view. After a lifetime of considering the evidence, a growing number of this elite conclude now that the universe really does explain itself, and that we are well on our way to wrapping our minds around the explanations.

By his own account, the evolutionary biologist and entomologist Edward O. Wilson was raised in a strong Protestant tradition. As his career in biology progressed, his empirical knowledge of the natural world began to confound the Christian doctrine of his youth. Although loath to turn from the Southern Baptist culture which formed his spiritual bedrock, he grew increasingly unsettled about his faith. Laboring in the trenches of scientific research for many decades, he digested ever more "hard" evidence. And finally—and reluctantly—he brought himself to accept the final analysis: to create and sustain the universe, no gods were needed after all. It happened "all by itself."

Much earlier, Charles Darwin, our founding modern secularist, bowing to his wife's deep Christianity, kept under wraps for almost *thirty years* his revolutionary theory of natural selection. Only in 1859 did he finally publish his monumental findings and their implications. In the end, risking a social pummeling at the hands of his contemporaries, he let the truth flow free, and declared publicly what writer George Levine calls his "enchanted secularity." The late evolutionary geologist Stephen Jay Gould, noting that many of Darwin's contemporaries criticized the theory of evolution as pessimistic, "even nihilist," has declared it instead to be "positive and exhilarating:"

> "It teaches us that the meaning of our lives cannot be read passively from the works of nature, but that we must struggle, think, and construct that meaning for ourselves."[75]

The contemporary critic Adam Gopnik pays modern homage to Darwin as "a skeptical materialist who had proved that the forms of life were shaped by history, not by a supervising mind."[76]

The Be-ist Within

Bolstered by the new evidence about the real nature of ourselves and the universe, perhaps we, like some of our leading contemporary thinkers, can "dare to be true." Perhaps we can face squarely the radical notion that the existence which *actually* presents itself to us is the only authentic truth. On the strength of its authenticity, it has the power to inspire us more deeply than any hypothetical version of it we have considered in the past. As adults, we think of ourselves as insisting on the truth. We think we are wary of exaggeration or over-emphasis, and of understatement or omission. We think we are open to freshness, simplicity, "cutting through." But are we really? If we *do* dare to be true, we may sense that we have come full circle: returned to a natural understanding that "hard" reality is all there is—and that its scope is immense, cosmic, more than worthy of a lifetime of full attention.

In leaving metaphysics behind, we may truly mourn the loss of the *idea* of "otherness" (much as children do when catching on to Santa Claus). The pain of forsaking a church, like the pain of outgrowing any phase of life which carries powerful associations (our childhood, our college years), is part of our own evolution, like the shedding of skin, the casting off of the outgrown shell, the spreading of wings. We look back with deep affection and nostalgia on the faded Little League uniform; the smocked Polly Flinders dress; the low-riding khaki safari shorts with the boxers showing underneath; the sexy satin prom dress. And with more awe, on the cathedrals and temples and mosques of the past, masterworks by grown men and women who still lived in an age of illusion, but whose legacy of aspiration and belief and imagination and prowess amazes us still.

But in compensation for our "loss," we are newly aware of the powers and senses and feelings in *ourselves,* and of the extraordinary fact of our awareness itself: the amazing consortium of abilities and consciousness that is made possible by our own brain (our mind) and body, and the power it holds to give us the opportunity for a rich and satisfying life. We find that *reality* plays to our strength – what is best and highest in us, most capable, most energetic, most enterprising, feistiest, most open and curious, most *alive*. Be-ism may restore to us our native clarity and sanity, our humor and our humility. Through it we may pave the way to a *secular* state of grace.

When will we dare to *declare* our secularity? When Sam Harris' book *The End of Faith* was published in 2004, a blurb on the cover quoted science writer Natalie Angier: "Harris writes what a sizable number of us think, but few are willing to say." Why do we find it wrong or uncomfortable or provocative to assert a secular view of existence? Why are we apologetic, speaking in low tones, checking behind us? Is our reticence rational, honorable? Our position is not *personal*; it is philosophical, a framework for facing the universe. We do not need to flaunt it—just express it, as a matter of course. It is what we really think. How do we *legitimize* a concept that is so basic, so self-evident—yet viewed as so subversive? If we don't lead the way, who will? If we do take a secular stand, will we be in the vanguard of the new thinking—charter members of the first truly enlightened generation in the history of humankind? If we say yes, perhaps we could explain ourselves this way:

We feel compelled to synchronize how we *think* about life and existence with our *actual experience of and knowledge about* life and existence. We want to advance our understanding of how the real world works, and come up with new solutions to enhance the well-being of humans and the greater world, and we have just one lifetime to do our part. We have a powerful and innate love of life and existence. We want to be strong and helpful and civil, in our way and in our time. We have confidence that if we are conscientious, our *good* nature can prevail: our good sense, good actions, good ideas, good taste, good will. We want to show a new kind of courage and fortitude by taking on—and moving beyond—the seemingly intractable, outmoded ideas and institutions of the past.

We honor and take to heart what the long practice of religion has taught us about *human* aspirations, hopes and fears, for that is the true story of religion and its role in human history. But the old religions and habits of thought which used to sustain us at so many levels, now – instead—seem to undermine deeply our ability to tend well the orchards and enjoy fully the fruits of the real universe. The world is round, but our minds—which start out round – have been flattened by indoctrination. Now that we are beginning to grasp how exceedingly complex reality actually is, we can put aside the speculative and imaginary explanations, and instead focus on and savor and marvel at what we *actually* have. It is much more than we realized.

In a reality-based life, our purpose is to strive for the *optimal* (which is achievable), rather than for some *ideal* (which is not). Our religious heritage tried to make us "Pilgrims of the Absolute."[77] Our new knowledge of the amazing real world beckons us instead to be "Pilgrims of the Possible." Rather than strive for an unattainable ideal, we instead become more practical, and aim for the best we can achieve. Rather than relying on "god" for help, we rely on each other. We hold a powerful *faith,* but it is in *ourselves and each other.* Humankind faces troubles, but some of them are avoidable or solvable by us. Even if, in the hubbub of a society which still embraces religion and old beliefs, we have no love for "the fight" for secularity, we owe it to ourselves to hold out for the truth. We can reassert our autonomy and insist on exercising our good will. Our own age is as good as any age that has gone before. Facing the universe squarely, embracing its facts and realities and harnessing them to improve the human condition and the health of the planet, we have the power to transform it into the best age in human history.

Go Fresh

When we are young we love myth and magic, and indulge our imagination with romantic idols and lofty ideals: fairy princesses and superheroes, Barbie dolls and Ninja warriors, dreams of power and glory. But once we are grown, we discover that true beauty and joy and satisfaction arrive in the form of a real live friend or mate or child of our own – unpredictable, complicated, flawed, but acutely real and incomparably precious to us. Authenticity, genuineness, realness touch us deeply and move us profoundly. The sounder our grounding in reality, the better able we are to distinguish between the real and the phony, and the less we are willing to tolerate show or falseness. Our affinity for *reality* is seldom considered or described, yet it is the subtext of all our fantasies and imaginary happy endings: to "live happily ever after." In a healthy person, this affinity for real existence knows no bounds. It is probably the most powerful force within us.

Remember Tom Hanks in the film "Cast Away"? A great parable about our unquenchable zest for life, and our overriding love, also, for our fellow man, a friend—even if we have to settle for "Wilson," a volleyball with magic marker eyes and smile.) We love life more than fear death. We don't want it to end: we don't want to miss out on what comes next.

What if astronomers warned us that the Earth was about to be obliterated by a giant asteroid?[78] Imagine the power of the nostalgia we would feel for our extraordinary existence. The affinity for life drives us forward, not just to survive, but to thrive. Be-ism is simply the recognition and embrace of this inborn positive impulse towards life; the acceptance that each life has a beginning and an end; and above all, immense gratitude for the fortune of being able to experience existence itself—for better and worse—in the better-than-any-fiction Real World.

※ ※ ※

In 2005 in a rural New England town an enterprising young Lebanese immigrant and his young Mexican wife put all their small savings into a new business in a tiny corner store in the village, where they offer fresh gelato and smoothies, homemade baba ganoush and tabouli, exquisitely prepared and cheerfully served. Their handsome freshly-painted sign announces the name of their shop: "GO FRESH." So far, their business is growing nicely. Perhaps we have something to learn from them about the future, and how we all should be thinking about it, and doing something about it.

The earth turns. The sun "rises"—the amazing sun, its heat and light the generator of life itself. We face the day. And a new secular age has dawned. It is just that it has not quite yet dawned on *us*. Now is the time to open our eyes wide and pay attention. We are embarking (knowingly or not) on a great supra-version, a process of turning the human world "right side up" for the first time in history. We are inexorably pushing forward the knowledge frontier, "getting real." Call it Be-ism or what you will, a secular view, grounded in reality, is sure to open to us an ever clearer view of existence – no longer through the dark glass of old beliefs, but truly face to face.

PART II

The Job and the Manual

(A 1ˢᵗ Draft)

Chapter 9

The Good Wolf

An old tribal grandfather and his granddaughter were sitting by the fire under the infinite stars above the plain. The grandfather seemed more quiet than usual, so the girl asked, "Grandfather, are you all right?"

He looked up at the sky and answered, "I am struggling, granddaughter, because there is a fight going on in my head and in my heart."

She asked, "What is the fight about, grandfather?"

He replied, "This fight is between two wolves inside me. One wolf is full of anger, envy, sorrow, regret, greed, arrogance, self-pity, guilt, resentment, inferiority and entitlement. The other wolf is full of joy, humor, serenity, love, hope, humility, kindness, generosity, courage and strength."

The girl was silent for a moment. Then she looked up and asked, "Grandfather, which wolf do you think will win?"

After a silence, the old man answered, "The one I feed, granddaughter. The one I feed."

--from a Native American legend

The Basics (or What to Tell the Kids)

What is the job, the game plan of life, for a secular believer—a Be-ist? How do we write "the manual"? Who can know for sure. But going on our experience so far, we start by penciling in, "No pain, no gain." Approaching the how-to subject warily—and knowing that no two lists would look alike—consider for a start the following (admittedly random) list of basics:

Start the day fresh.
"Hear what the morning says, and believe that." [79]

Look around. Pay attention to whomever and whatever is present (at home, in the office, on the subway, on the sidewalk). That is existence—at least for everyday purposes. And then, from time to time, stand back and take a higher, wider, deeper look. Track the cosmos. Practice, in the phrase of the late Polish writer Ryzard Kapuscinski, "the art of noticing." (Kapuscinski "reminds us again and again how profound our senses are—what a foundation they are for everything we call intellect—and how little we remember to use them.")[80]

Just think.
"Men fear thought as they fear nothing else on earth – more than ruin—more even than death.... Thought is subversive and revolutionary.... Thought is great and swift and free, the light of the world, and the chief glory of man."

Bertrand Russell (1872-1970), British author, mathematician and philosopher

To think. The hardest part. We *process* our experience and knowledge. We consider well, then decide, what we *really* believe about "whatever comes up." When the situation or information changes, we consider anew and decide again. It is up to us to play fair with knowledge and experience (don't fool ourselves), and to use them for good ends.

To achieve more subtlety and keenness in our observation and thought, we practice detachment. Turn off the radio, the iPod. Find a virtual or real mountain top or a quiet place. Take "ourselves" out of the equation, to see more clearly things as they are.

Use "we".
Try "getting to **we.**" (And to "our" and "us.") We hear a married friend speak of "my" children, "my" kitchen, "my" house. Or a colleague, after a group project or collaboration, refer to "my" idea, "my" solution, "my" plan. Time to get past "I." (It used to

be a standard rule of good form: do not begin any piece of writing or speaking with "I.")

Honor others.
As we "insist on ourselves," honor others. Appreciate their merits and accomplishments. Respect their autonomy—their "space"—as we would have them respect ours.

Keep an open mind.
Seek out new people and ideas and places and pursuits. Cultivate every chance to exchange ideas and information and views. Relish the difference.

Todd Pittinsky, a social psychologist at Harvard University, is pursuing new research on *allophilia*: *liking* for other groups (rather than merely *tolerating* differences), and the behavior it inspires. Allophilia, too, is a common human characteristic, found in people for whom difference in itself is alluring, people who tend to "accentuate the positive."[81]

Consider authority.
In exercising and in answering to authority, be fair and scrupulous. Authority carries an adult burden.

Think again about "entitlement".
How about a revised concept:

All humans (and other species, too) have *needs* and *aspirations*. But in the cosmic picture, what is our *right* to life or safety or consideration—for instance in the face of an earthquake, or a tsunami, or an accidental plane crash, or a stray bullet? Who has the special standing to grant, or demand, a *human* right?

Customary or *legal* "rights," on the other hand, are a human construct, which continue to be upheld only as long as we continue to demand them. Even the most basic "rights" we insist upon—the right to our own thoughts or to the inviolacy of our own body—are not so universally agreed upon that, as a society, we can risk inattention to them: weighing them, codifying them, and explicitly asserting them. (Repressive societies refuse to acknowledge these "rights.")[82]

Take time.
    In the "developed" world, the normal span of a human life is well above seventy years (above eighty, in some nations). Each day and year is one small segment of a long lifetime. If we live in the expectation (not unrealistic, for most of us) that life will be long, we are aware of more breathing room for the present. We acknowledge that there is ample time to plan and carry out plans in the years ahead. We can damp down the anxious sense of a headlong race to the future (or to the finish) which our fast-moving, hyper-caffeinated, time-stressed culture seems to foster. We can moderate the caffeine; occasionally turn off the Blackberry, the cellphone, the computer, the TV. We can get more sleep. In doing so, we *increase* our life expectancy—and at the same time give the people around us a break (for instance our children or our co-workers). "Hypeness" is highly contagious, infects everyone in its force field. If we each live as though expecting a long life, perhaps the group will slow down a bit too, and society itself become more civil and enjoyable. Life is just Mondays and Tuesdays – why not savor them as we go?

Simplify.
    Take Thoreau to heart: "Simplify. Simplify."
    Spend time on the land.
    Make do with less.
    In an age of complexity we are deprived of simplicity. It is hard to untangle our lives. The magazine rack offers *Real Simple* at the checkout line. The slow food and voluntary simplicity movements, the back-to-the-land and environmental movements, converge to push for "relocalization." [83] The world turns to yoga. Spas and retreats promise a respite. But we can get close to the earth, the sky, the outdoors, by just appreciating the ground

beneath us and the sky above. "The mottled clouds, like scraps of wool, steeped in the light are beautiful."[84]

Consider the innovative concept of The Farm School, a working organic farm in northern Massachusetts, with Jersey dairy herd, work horses, chickens, pigs, goats, a huge vegetable garden, a maple sugaring operation, a forestry program. Here, urban and suburban school children come from all corners of the state for a few days of real farm experience: rise at dawn, milk the cows, weed the garden, feed the goats, collect the eggs, muck out the pigpen, feast on the fresh produce. And look up at the stars at night, from the quiet rural hilltop. See how it feels.

To stay grounded in a complex fast-moving world is a high goal, not so easy to attain.

Work.

Work is good. (*Over*work, or work that inflicts unreasonable damage, is not.)

Uncoerced, we often *choose* work. We tend to be naturally industrious, at least some of the time. From work comes competency, productivity, engagement, the satisfaction of being useful and sharing the load. And the earnings, of course.

Try for dignity.

During days of relative safety and comfort and prosperity, we seldom face the need to take the measure of our own inner strength. But perhaps easy times are getting in the way of our best selves. Paradoxically, it may *require* hardship for us to achieve true dignity. Extreme adversity may unlock a cache of courage and calm and humor we never knew we owned. (Or not.) It seems to be in the cancer wards, the military hospitals, the refugee camps of the world where we encounter the most extraordinary examples of human strength, endurance, forbearance, and irony: our fellow humans put to the test, and discovering in themselves resources to allow them to survive and endure with grace and class. A cheerful face, in spite of everything.

In her 2007 documentary *Rain in a Dry Land*, Emmy award-winning filmmaker Anne Makepeace follows two Somali "Bantu" families from refugee camps in northern Kenya (where they fled war in Somalia in the early 1990s) to their resettlement homes in Springfield, MA and Atlanta, GA. In the winter of 2003, two Bantu women—each the mother of several young children, some of whom vanished during the chaos of the war— arrive in the USA with their remaining children. They have endured unimaginable wartime trauma, then a decade of struggle for survival in the camps, never with the opportunity to become literate even in their own language. Suddenly they are transported, virtually overnight, into a welfare-level subsistence in the unimaginably (to them) alien culture of urban America. (What would *we* do, if the coin were flipped? If we arrived traumatized and destitute and illiterate in a modern city on the other side of the planet, and were placed in an inner-city apartment where we knew no one, could not speak the language, could not support ourselves?)

In the film, the women reveal the power of human dignity: they have an inner poise, a force of character, a rock-like steadiness, which enables them still to "smile at the good," while embarking on the mind-boggling challenge of acculturating to their new life. They try to learn English. They get jobs. They dress in bold brilliant fabrics. They laugh a lot. (Sometimes they gripe, too. They're only human.) They take exceptional care of their children. As their hosts, we will try to provide them with economic and material opportunities. But we can learn a lot from them, too— about strength and dignity and solidarity and style. They have brought with them something of high value. Are we open to receiving it?

※ ※ ※

The Job

Our success as people lies in the balance we achieve in carrying out, to our best ability, the job—the diverse functions and "mission" of life. Our practices, taken as a whole, comprise the evolving form of human society itself, integral with the existence around us. They draw on a combination of our intrinsic nature and our "learned" nurture, translated into pragmatic action and behavior which enable us to survive and thrive in the real world, among the millions of species with which we share it. In thinking about "practice"—and about the internal forces that drive our actions and thought and feeling—five human motivations and aspirations come to mind. "The five" are necessarily arbitrary: they overlap and oversimplify. But perhaps they can bring focus to a view of the "job" of a secular life. Our vocations and motivations often are obscure to us because they are *in* us—too close to observe. More alert to their influence, maybe we can do better at optimizing them in good times, and rebooting them in bad times.

The following chapters will address these five areas of practice:

Learn and Teach: Acquire knowledge and share it
Act: Prove we exist
Do Good: Advance the well-being of our fellow humans
Do Better: Advance the well-being of the natural world
Have Fun (and Give Thanks): Reflect on, enjoy and celebrate existence

We always—since the beginnings of human language and culture—have found our own behavior and motivations a subject of endless fascination. All the five human pursuits mentioned above are the focus of significant—even urgent – research today, in the "hard" and the "soft" sciences, and the humanities as well. Best-selling books and the popular media and the serious journals and university graduate courses vie for our attention, each with new findings and theories and speculation on learning, on physical activity and engagement, on improving human welfare, on saving the planet, on the pursuit of happiness, on a workable philosophy of life. Here there is no scholarly treatise on the five pursuits — just an overview, and a short consideration of what might constitute good practice for each of them.

Chapter 10

Learn and Teach: Acquire knowledge and share it

Through the eons of human existence, people have pursued knowledge and applied it for their own purposes. We are no different. But as suggested earlier, our *circumstances* are different, because of the enormous gains we have made—relatively recently—in learning "how the world works" and in spreading this revolutionary knowledge throughout human society, or at least being able to do so easily. In the last few decades we have developed technology with extraordinary capability to identify and record and process and store huge amounts of information of all types: scientific, social, economic, medical, demographic, to name a few. Nanotechnology allows us to "see" and manipulate and understand the smallest of the small: to splice genes, to capture and then "take apart" cosmic dust particles from millions of miles into deep space. [85] Mammoth computer servers and search engines and telecommunications systems make the new knowledge (as well as the old) "democratic": cheap and easily available, at least to all who have moderate economic means and live in "open" societies. Information is harvested and put to use in thousands of ways. (Sometimes it even is information about us—with or without our knowledge or consent—and it will be used to predict or influence what we buy or how we vote or whom we marry.)

Barring cataclysmic events, the rush to knowledge –and to disseminate knowledge—probably will continue unabated, at least in relatively open human societies. The more knowledge and reasoning power we have, the more we can enjoy and appreciate the diversity of the world for its own sake; and perhaps the more we know, the more likely it is that *curiosity and affection* will replace *fear-and-loathing* in our global society. Knowledge is power: economic power, political power, social power. And close behind (or in advance of?) the quest for power is the apparently insatiable human "need to know":   knowledge for its own sake. With the formidable new tools at our disposal, the cosmos itself is the limit.

The recent gains in knowledge are a key factor—really *the* key factor—in the movement toward a new secularity. It does not take a book or a polemic to deliver the news of a huge worldwide contemporary movement by humankind toward acquiring new knowledge; likewise, a huge worldwide movement toward improving education for all. Human aspiration drives these movements: for a better life and a healthier planet, and the ever present desire simply to *know more*. We take the fact for granted. To call it a "vocation" is stating the obvious. But isn't it worthy of attention as a phenomenon, in itself, which is perhaps uniquely human: a phenomenon which is possible because of the extraordinary capability of the human brain to acquire and process and use information and ideas; and to devise clever and powerful ways of communicating information and ideas to others, plus mechanisms (books, computers) for storing them for future use.

We live in a culture which *assumes* the high value of existing knowledge and the desirability of more knowledge. We know that knowledge comes from study and observation and experiment and experience. We admire and respect and rely on experts, who have more mastery than us of a given subject or field or occupation. We understand that although "knowledge is power," *wisdom* is the ability to synthesize and apply knowledge well to new human situations.

Our whole concept of, and system of, education is grounded in the assumption that a broad base of knowledge is really *necessary* for a satisfactory life. In democratic societies, we agree on the premise that all citizens are not only entitled, but required, to avail themselves of the opportunity to acquire a broad foundation of knowledge.

In pre-industrial traditional societies, education is often unattainable but an incomparably precious commodity. The "Lost Boys" of Sudan, child refugees from their war-torn country, arrived in the 1990's in the USA and other host countries to start a new life; teenagers then, they settled in to their adopted new homes with one single-minded focus: education. Orphans, their credo is "Education Is My Mother and My Father."

In the past decade many of the Sudanis already have earned college degrees, and some are returning to Sudan to sponsor schools and hospitals; they hope eventually to be able to help lead their struggling country to a better life.[86] Writer David Chanoff explains more about the academic zeal of the Lost Boys:

"Professor Vivian Zamel [Professor of English at the University of Massachusetts] said, 'They don't rest easy.... The Sudanese are very disturbed by not knowing. Knowing how much they don't know disturbs them.'

For the Lost Boys, learning has become over the years a survival mechanism, not only an internalized value but a driving force. They, who were born into the most insular and static of cultures, have evolved into a community of sojourners, and as such they have acquired the sojourner's two most essential pieces of baggage. They understand, first, that knowledge is a portable commodity, to be gathered like gold at each stop along the way for use at the next. They have learned too that intelligence itself is the most dynamic of human characteristics....

Given what they have experienced, the death of families and friends, the long years of violence and deprivation, they might have been expected to have become aggressive and hard-shelled, violent in their own lives. Yet the opposite seems to be true. 'They are open, positive, optimistic,' as one of their teachers put it. 'Given that they grew up without any real adult guidance, it reaffirms something about what you hope human beings really are. It's like *Lord of the Flies* in reverse.'"[87]

Through support of universities and investment in public and corporate and governmental and non-profit research, we stimulate and reward (sometimes well, sometimes less well) the quest for new knowledge. We celebrate and reward *success* in advancing knowledge through media recognition and prizes and professional advancement and financial compensation. As thinkers, we cheer the announcement of new discoveries, and react with a visceral pleasure and a vicarious thrill (and maybe a twinge of envy) in learning that one of our fellows has just pushed the envelope of what was known before.

Perhaps, here, it is not of so much interest *why* we have this strong affinity for knowledge; rather, it is the fact of our affinity that matters in itself. It is in our interest to be aware of this fact: to recognize and appreciate the desire for knowledge as a "given," an internal force which motivates us in a positive direction—a force which we will cultivate wisely and use well, if we want to optimize our life. In recognizing the force of our own drive to acquire more knowledge, we sense that we are programmed not just to survive but to thrive, and that (presumably) our fellow humans are endowed with a like desire for an optimal life. Does a recognition of this innate motivation suggest that we might raise the knowledge bar, for ourselves and the human community? That perhaps, rather than settling for "No Child Left Behind," we might push instead for "*Every Child to Excel*"?

When society comes to recognize more clearly that knowledge—not degrees or credentials, but *knowledge itself*—is the crucial tool for achieving the best life, we might start to invest considerably more effort and imagination in the whole culture of education. Taking into account the latest neuroscience and social science and technology, we might think freshly about the entire process of education, and how it might be incorporated optimally into the whole life of a person. What is the optimal way of achieving balance *throughout* our life: a healthy dynamic balance among learning, action, work, contribution, self-expression and leisure? Why does an affluent society prescribe that we dedicate almost eighteen years of our youth—our entire youth—to *education*, with a minor role for other pursuits? Are the other pursuits deemed less important? Are young people thought not to be capable of them?

And how about the physical environment we provide for this extremely long-drawn-out "education" of our young? If we truly esteem *knowledge* (as we claim to), why is it that so many of our modern schools resemble large storage units or warehouses: shallow or massive concrete boxes with sealed plate-glass windows, typically surrounded by pavement. Budget materials. Low ceilings. Lightweight minimalist furniture. Flat hard surfaces. Little elegance or richness or inspiration. Would it be fair to expect, in an increasingly secular age, in an affluent and educated society, that the schools would be the *temples* of modern culture? That the best resources available would be mustered to make them as sound, beautiful and inspiring as the cathedrals and temples and mosques of our "old" religion-based culture. That they would be designed and cared for, and cared about, as the *best* place to be—especially considering that the young of our species, our "children" (from age three to twenty-one!), spend most of their daytime life in them, many more waking hours than they spend at home. Curiously, in earlier times (the late nineteenth and earlier twentieth century), schools—public and private—tended to boast elegant buildings well designed and built to last, on beautiful sites, landscaped with shady trees and gracious lawns and even lavish gardens. Often they were built and donated and supported by wealthy entrepreneurs. (Likewise, the free libraries, established coast to coast by gifts from Andrew Carnegie.) What happened? What does modern school architecture and siting suggest about our *real* attitude to education, and its priority in our culture?

As natural as it is to love learning, so it goes for teaching: all of us do both, in many contexts and diverse ways. But maybe we don't stand back and consider that fact, and how integral it is to passing along knowledge from one generation to the next and among contemporaries of the same generation. Teaching is just "there." But absolutely crucial to the well-being and maintenance— let alone advancement—of society. We know we can rethink and improve our technologies and methods and approaches for doing it better. Natalie Angier, the science writer, visits the Academy of

Science, "the almost sneakily rigorous high school magnet science program in Loudoun County, Virginia....a visit to which is almost enough to make you wish you were back in high school." (Not only are individual schools ratcheting up their science teaching: the percentage of American high school students taking physics courses in 2007 was at an all-time high, and the number of bachelor's degrees in physics climbed 31 percent since 2000.) Lamenting our wrong perception of science, Angier quotes Eugene Levy, a professor of physics and astronomy at Rice University: "Science is, or should be, about the world, not about science. But for too many students, science has been presented as a large series of manipulations that they rarely understand or connect to the reality around them," whereas in fact, "the world is understandable, ... rational inquiry can lead to understanding, and ...there's rarely an excuse to say understanding is beyond them."[88]

Teaching is by nature satisfying work, for teacher and student. We are innately programmed to do it. And if in our times it is *not* satisfying and exciting in practice, maybe we could be taking a closer look.

* * *

The Practice

What is good "practice" for a Be-ist, in the face of this flood of knowledge and with these powerful tools available for acquiring, sharing and using it? Perhaps the first good practice is to be open to all information that comes our way. Build on our "base" knowledge: what we have learned through our twelve or sixteen or umpteen years of school; through experience; through self-education in subjects of interest and relevance; through tuning in to the world around us. Make a concerted effort to understand better what is happening in our own world and in the greater cosmos, or at least those parts of it which spark our curiosity. If we have an opportunity and a skill, advance the knowledge further: go where someone maybe has not gone before. We may not be a particle physicist or a PhDs in philosophy or a cutting edge neurosurgeons, but we can use our mind to the max. Think hard. Show intellectual courage. Pursue a new idea (or one that is new to us) if we have one. Applying the full power of our mind to a subject of interest—through research, analysis, intuition, imagination, integration—we may arrive at a *new* synthesis, a sudden "aha" moment, a convergence of ideas, facts and theory that coalesces and suddenly becomes evident. (Perhaps no one has reached that point before. The world *may* be waiting.)

Acquire knowledge at the expense of other less productive activities—or non-activities. *Choose* to be well-informed. Exercise mental rigor. Challenge our brain to keep it functioning well: commit facts to memory, learn a poem, study a piece in the science or literature section of the newspaper or magazine. Read about Uganda or mosquito larvae. Vet our reading and radio and TV and internet habits: be a little more challenging to ourselves. Take a break from the sports pages or the celebrity news or the stock market quotes or the opinion blogs or the porn. Recognize non-productive or counter-productive information addictions if we have them, and get a grip. Be fair, by paying real attention to other points of view, recognizing that the people who hold them are to some degree (perhaps more than we think) just other people like us. Don't make the mistake of assuming we are special (or at the other extreme, unworthy) in the "knowledge" department. Our information or facts or ideas or views may or may not be special, but each of us is just one more human, tackling the challenges and building on the achievements of everyone who came before us. (Posterity, later, can pronounce on the brilliance of our insight or the scope of our knowledge.)

What about *sharing* knowledge? Here we encounter the broad domains of education and communications (journalism, the media, the publishing business, information technology). There is a "macro" question: how do we disseminate all the hard-won knowledge we have accumulated—the fruit of hundreds of generations of human curiosity and effort and imagination and ingenuity—to all people, across all societies and cultures, so they will have an equal opportunity to benefit from it? There is a "micro" question: will you share with any other person a single idea you had as a result of reading this particular book? There are the opposite inclinations, as well: to refuse new knowledge ("Don't confuse me with the facts"); and to hoard knowledge (as "power"). A rigorous look at these issues is way beyond the scope of this book. But through them all we see a common theme: we are strongly, innately disposed to seek knowledge, and at least in a limited way, to pass along what we know. We get a high degree of satisfaction from both endeavors: learning and teaching. We feel a thrill of discovery at every new fact or idea, and a vicarious thrill—perhaps as intense as the original—in the flash of understanding that we see in the person to whom we pass it on.

Great societal questions loom, about how to get knowledge "up to speed"—how to structure education and communications systems to inform the general population about "old" knowledge and the latest discoveries in biology and physics, history and music, economics and anthropology. To play a role in pursuing and disseminating true information for beneficial purposes, in any aspect of research and education and the "knowledge" business, must be a worthy lifetime practice for any of us.

And there is the growing challenge of *too much* knowledge: an enormous overload of information, not only about what has been discovered and what has happened already, but about what is coming our way, what is in store. We must process the incoming data and plan ahead based on the forecasts and predictions of the next ten days' weather, and of the next ten decades of global warming. We know the gender of, and can detect the defects in our babies before they are born; and the demographers and economists warn us that that those babies will have to work longer and harder than we did, in an entirely transformed economy, to support us in our old age. We can estimate the likelihood that we and our sons and daughters will get cancer or Alzheimer's disease; or the timetable on which the economy of China will overtake that of the USA. Among all the predictions there is a great range in the degree of certainty—and of course, many trends and events which we cannot accurately predict. (Where will the next large earthquake strike in the US? Will there ever be peace in the Middle East? *Will* the Cubs ever win the World Series?)

The "trick" of processing all the available information, or selecting efficiently from the vast pool what we really need or desire to know, is a momentous challenge. In order to maintain our mental health, we each must master the art of managing a *global* information system—readily at our disposal through the internet and many other media—while still retaining the art of living in the moment. Google, and the cybernet in all its forms, are of inestimable help. The scale of the task is greater every moment, but our brains—our truly extraordinary brains—so far seem to be able not only to respond, but to look forward to still more input. We are future oriented. Like the gleaming new Institute of Contemporary Art which opened recently on the Boston harborfront, we seem to be cantilevered toward the future. The secret is to be able to hold the extended weight: to be sufficiently anchored in the present to sustain our flight to the future—and to commit to doing all we can to assure that the future is "light enough to bear."

※ ※ ※

Chapter 11

Act: To Prove We Exist

To exist is to be in action. We're not sloths. We're not lumps on logs. We *live* life—we don't just think about it. ("Just thinking about it" can bring us to a functional standstill, as we discover after a bout of excessive introspection or fixation or angst, or a period of forced inactivity.) We get zest and satisfaction out of *doing*—especially doing something we have a knack for and an interest in, something which seems productive or at least amusing or entertaining or exciting. We naturally want to *do well*. We are biologically programmed for it, in intricate and extraordinarily complex ways.

The human body is a contraption with millions of working parts (trillions, if you count cells, gazillions if you count molecules). It functions as a complex animated *corpus* of electrical charges, chemical reactions, fluid dynamics, mechanical actions, heat exchange, and related (and equally mind-boggling) forces and processes. Its multiple integrated systems keep us continually energized, breathing, moving, feeling, thinking, and reproducing ourselves: the product of billions of years of evolution. Amazing, that in addition to all this ongoing action, there still is energy left over (sometimes a lot) with which to *live* life: "energy to burn."

The Greek ideal was a sound mind in a sound body: their icon—in gleaming marble—was the elegantly sculpted muscular form of the thinking athlete. In all cultures the same ideal holds, today. As player or observer, we find extreme pleasure in the strength, skill, grace, speed, resilience, cleverness and endurance of the gymnast, the dancer, the soccer player, the swimmer, the football player, the snow boarder. The action comes across to us as dynamic, exciting, supremely graceful at moments, sometimes awesome. Athletes are prominent among our star (and mostly generously paid) celebrities—a good measure of how much we value and admire them and what they do. They are our action surrogates. Physical contests provide a healthy outlet for the aggression and competitiveness which are innate in us, and probably are necessary for a healthy dynamic society. Of course their activity is not a *substitute* for our own; and professional athletes' competitions, their personal values, and the commercial environment in which they exist are no more "pure" than any other commercial or human enterprise. Yet, on balance, spectator sports may play a significantly positive role in modern society, feeding vicariously our need for rivalry and action.

Are prosperous modern cultures in danger of overlooking—or of having forgotten amidst the cushioned ease and convenience and frenetic time pressure of modern life—the vital importance to us of physical exertion, and the cultivation of physical skill and strength? Since "progress" has relieved us of much of the ordinary use of our hands and feet, we end up going out of our way (to the health club or the gym) to experience the awake-and-aliveness that comes from physical exercise. Paying out-of-pocket for a physical workout (the health club, the Pilates class) reinforces our sense of it as an "extra," rather than a basic requirement for life.

Health issues aside, do we value in itself the satisfaction (a "given" in past times) of achieving something by our own physical effort—even the smallest effort, such as taking the stairs, not the elevator; mowing the lawn; knitting a sweater by hand; hand beating the eggs? How do we view physical *work*? Is it thought of as a "good" anymore; or instead, as socially demeaning, undesirably onerous, to be avoided? (Then we pay twice: once to have the yard service mow the lawn, and once to join the health club or the Pilates class.) Have we thought this through? If we continue to devalue physical work, we also fail to acquire or master the (often considerable) skills and strength which it requires. These tend to be practical skills (and muscle power) which could be of general use— even enjoyment—to us, and make us better prepared for the exigencies of an unpredictable life. In a predicament or emergency, are we self-sufficient—or do we rely on someone *else* knowing what to do? Often practical work requires only minimal physical exertion, but even so, are we inclined to avoid learning and doing it?

Virtually every recent study of health and well-being shows conclusively the benefits of vigorous physical exertion, and not only for the body. The studies also reveal vital links between physical activity and the function of the brain and mind. In November 2007, science journalists report that, more than any single "brain exercise" program late in life (such a memorizing poetry or playing bridge), "one form of training has been shown to maintain and improve brain health—physical exercise;" that "exercise improves what scientists call 'executive function,'...basic functions like processing speed, response speed and working memory.... Exercise also is associated with a reduced risk of dementia late in life." [89] In January 2008, another new headline about the mind-body link: "New research suggests that we think not just with our brains, but with our bodies." The new work has built on decades of research by neuroscientists and linguists into human movement and gesture, especially after the discovery in 1995 of "mirror neurons" that respond when we see someone else performing an action, as if we ourselves were performing it.

> "A series of studies, the latest published in November [2007], has shown that children can solve math problems better if if they are told to use their hands while thinking.... The term most often used to describe this new model of mind is "embodied cognition."[90]

The motto of the "embodied cognition" lab at the University of Wisconsin: "Ago ergo cogito." I act, therefore I think.

The evidence in favor of physical action is in and growing. But changing the attitude and habits of a sedentary life, let alone a "catered" life (if we are so fortunate), is not at all easy. It requires much more effort than simply "registering" the new facts about the benefits of exercise. Habits are hard to break, for one individual at a time. Cultural habits are much harder to change, because the large group has so much more inertia and gravitas—is so much more vested in the status quo. However, once an old pattern does "tip" in a new direction (pushed by a society-wide sense of urgency about a problem, and a communal decision to tackle it), the rest of us follow more readily: the group starts to invest in the new direction or the new behavior. The norm changes. It's easier to run two miles every morning if everyone is doing it. We or our teenager will mow the lawn if the neighbor and the neighbor's teenagers are out mowing too. Or if everyone is taking the stairs. Society makes changes to accommodate the beneficial new behavior: an in-house health club; company-sponsored marathon teams; how-to classes in gardening or cooking or auto maintenance. The fast-food industry reduces trans-fats and offers salads. The benefits of the new behavior start to show up: less illness, more productivity, more readiness to "jump in" in emergencies of various sorts, more well-being.

Even in a relatively tamed society, we still do face a greater or lesser share of real physical action, and are tested accordingly: our prowess, strength and endurance; and the wits, skill and intelligence which the work requires. The weather conscripts us into battle against snow or flood, hurricane or forest fire. There are the surrogate battlefields, sports being the most obvious. Because the taming and civilizing never is complete, we as a people face and combat often-overwhelming physical challenges in blighted urban neighborhoods and rural areas of poverty, rife with drug abuse, domestic and gang violence, entrenched subcultures of deprivation, desperation and hopelessness. Our police and firefighters and search-rescue teams and emergency personnel face real danger at home. Our soldiers and marines and sailors and airmen and relief workers face real war in other parts of the world. Construction and manufacturing and health and transportation workers, farmers, fishermen and loggers daily face dangerous physical risks on the job.

But so many of us meanwhile live a relatively safe and comfortable life, buffered by "civilization" from the survival struggles of our ancestors, or those of our struggling local and global neighbors. Seeking more challenge and excitement, we embrace risk for its own sake: NASCAR racing, hang-gliding, para-sailing, extreme skiing, storm surfing, hurricane chasing. We still are coming to terms with our safety and comforts. No doubt we are wise not to take them for granted: ultimately prudent to somehow make ourselves "ready for anything" in case the civilized buffer erodes or vanishes overnight. (Remember the fad for "Survival Kits" and manuals—some facetious and some for real—in the aftermath of 9/11?)

Paradoxically, perhaps, the impact of the Al Qaeda attacks of 9/11/01, extreme and horrific, seems to have waked us up as a culture: turned us back, at least temporarily, into active players; made us realize that as a society we had fallen into the habit of standing on the sidelines, commenting and observing, and sometimes waiting impatiently to be served. The 2004 tsunami at Banda Aceh in Indonesia, and the ravages of Hurricane Katrina in New Orleans, catalyzed a similar response: they—for a time—brought us alive, re-engaged us in the world. Shaken by a crisis, we suddenly are alert, newly conscious of our surroundings, acutely aware of our own existence, moved to action. We are *more alive* than we were. It feels strange (unfamiliar), and ironically—considering the appalling damage suffered—it feels good, because we suddenly sense we are firing on all cylinders. Can we learn something important if we digest this lesson? Once we have known full "aliveness," how do we view a return to a more passive semi-life? If we realize that physical exertion itself will re-energize us and give us a heightened sense of existence, could we decide to be more active—and therefore more alive—*every* day? Does it take a tsunami or a bomb to wake us up and get us moving—a terrorist cabal or a geological upheaval? Or is it up to *us*.

* * *

The Practice

Maybe it is how we put our "extra" energy to use that determines the character and the caliber of our life. If so, how do we harness it, sustain it, optimize it in the service of our particular abilities and needs and desires? Again, there are no magic solutions, but just lessons gleaned from the cumulative experience of ourselves and our ancestors. Below are a few that may be worth considering.

Go with the strong suit.

Take inventory of our own natural abilities, our inherent strengths. What is the "us" about us that distinguishes us from our brother or friend or classmate or colleague? If we can't figure it out ourselves, ask them (at an appropriate moment). Listen to the assessment. It will at least be somewhere to start from. (Some humility may be in order—but also the candor to acknowledge our strengths.) And if we *are* a parent or a teacher or a colleague or a friend, take note of the abilities and leanings of our child or student or co-employee or friend, and enlist ourselves in their cause: consider how their talent and special traits could be put to use and how we might help, and follow through. Their thriving is a benefit to us and to the community

A key tenet of the emerging field of Positive Psychology is that "people become more engaged in activities that call on their inherent strengths. Everyone's strengths are different, so positive psychology helps people identify and draw on their most prominent ones, or their 'signature strengths.'" [91] If we are equipped for and attracted to a vocation, launch into it. Tune out the voices of "they" if they say nay. (Choose advisers carefully. Resist the pressure of unsolicited advice.) Do our own homework. Believe ourselves. Be a grownup. If we choose wrong at first, or if our choice does not work out, return to "Go" and try a different path. Avoid over-sensitivity to the world's *opinion* of what we do, either positive or negative—unless we are doing harm, of course. Anyone who has our interest at heart will want us to be productive and satisfied in our life.

Get around.

Take every chance to explore different pursuits and places. A variety of experience most likely will generate rewards of its own, and it will diversify our options for an occupation or avocation.

Keep an ear to the ground and eyes on the horizon. Find good teachers and look for good models. Try things out.

Move.
To say it again, the human body is an exceptionally fine-tuned machine. (Yes, yours too....) It is built for and needs regular active use. Otherwise it stiffens and sags and bloats and ossifies: a tremendous waste of good resources. The physical machine is highly integrated with our mental self: each is dependent on the other for optimum performance. So we must *move*. Run, dance, jog, stretch, play sports, dig the garden, mow the lawn, *rake* (don't blow) the leaves, walk briskly—stand up straight. Look alive. Strenuous exercise brings us awake, oxygenates the blood, energizes us, works off frustration or restlessness, wards off angst or the blues. Our body is "meant" to keep moving. And if the exertion is in the form of *work*, we accomplish something productive while honing our physique.

Get together.
Stay engaged, frequently and animatedly, with the people to whom we are drawn. Give them support and encouragement, as we accept it from them. Get together for dinner. Carve out time to talk and do things and go places together. Make a special effort for every rendezvous—at least to avoid the standard pitfalls: too many people? too loud music? too much distraction?
Take in firm hand the setting and the terms of our social life. Our special friends and colleagues are a rich treasure, and good times with them may well be our greatest pleasure in life. Why not optimize every encounter?

Be a player.
Pay attention to what is "in" and what is "out." Keep up with the standards and rules and social *mores* of our contemporaries and of the generations younger and older. If their language and music and dress—their obsessions and idols and

"attitude" and aspirations—are different from ours, think about it. Culture evolves. Each of us is somewhere in the mix. We remain a player if we participate. If we observe customs or attitudes or norms that disturb us because they seem destructive or dangerous, it's our obligation to speak up or show up. Ask good questions. Get involved. Communicate.

Our society is an endlessly fascinating dynamic exhibit of the role being played by "us" in the continuing drama of human existence. Each of us has a chance to affect it, for better or worse.

※ ※ ※

Chapter **12**

Do Good: Advance human well-being

What is "human well-being?"   What is "to do good"? How do we define the terms?   A grand and complicated topic, of course, subject to avid study and intense debate throughout human history, certainly continuing with vigor in the present.   First, "well-being:"

What is Human Well-being?

A fair question.   What is common to the people who thrive?   What are the pre-requisites and requirements for human joy, satisfaction and contentment?   What are the goods which bring us pleasure and fulfillment?   What *is* the happiness which we are supposed to be free to pursue?   Our own experience and common sense probably can provide a reasonable working list of the basic requirements.   Supplementing that, of course, is the monumental and ever-proliferating body of research and reporting and discussion and self-help literature on the subject.   But our own insight may well be more valuable than we realize.   (After all, "it's all about us.")   We defer to "experts."   Yet on a profoundly internal matter such as this – the subject of our own personal well-being—are we making an adequate effort to form our own view, apart from the research and experience and views and conclusions of "experts"?   Are we giving fair weight to our own experience and self-knowledge, as we read and listen to and process the views of others (including books like this....)?

Bypassing the experts, any "civilian" might include some or all of the following as *attributes of human well-being* (while not presuming such a list is all-inclusive):

1. **Safety:** freedom from harm, or *threat* of harm, to our life or physical or mental health.
2. Possession of, and the ability to obtain, adequate **food, clothing and shelter.**
3. **Physical and mental health:** good physical health, absence of pain or discomfort, and freedom from mental or emotional illness or impairment.
4. **Intactness:** freedom from physical injury, disfigurement, or significant anomaly impairing our function or appearance.
5. **Competency** for normal human tasks and functions, and awareness of this competency.
6. **Affection:** a mutually civil and affectionate social environment, where we like others and are aware of being liked in return by our "given" and our chosen society (mate, family, friends, colleagues, clients); and where we expect these bonds will continue and grow.
7. A **favorable physical environment:** with respect to space, light (including sunlight), temperature, moisture, noise, odor, orderliness, cleanliness, and design and scale of manmade elements such as buildings, transportation infrastructure, parks and recreational facilities.
8. **Freedom of action and movement:** wide choice, and control—as well as a sense of control—over our choice of where to go and what to do, including how much risk (or what extremes of action) we will undertake.
9. **Financial security:** the ability to meet our financial needs and wants now and in the future.
10. **Extra competency** in our area(s) of special skill and interest: achievement (in the extreme, making a breakthrough in our field), and expectation of future achievement.
11. **Access** to the greatly diverse goods of the world: the natural and manmade physical world; the arts and literature; the media; sports; cuisine and couture—all the beautiful and amusing and useful things the culture offers.
12. **A sense of oneness:** an awareness of being in harmony with, and fully alive in, the world.

A fair measure of how much *well-being* we have achieved is how *happy* we are. But what is "happiness?" Another great question in itself, which has all of us pondering, and the scientists hard at work.

Happiness

Happiness research "arrived" in the cognitive sciences with the new millennium. In 2000, the psychologist Martin Seligman of the University of Pennsylvania launched the study of "positive psychology," turning psychiatry for the first time (incredibly) to the serious study of *healthy* emotional life. Seligman has discovered that "engagement and the pursuit of meaning are much more predictive of life satisfaction than the pursuit of pleasure, and that externalities (e.g. weather, money, health, marriage, religion) together account for no more than eighteen per cent of the variance in life satisfaction."[92] The British economist Richard Layard, in *Happiness: Lessons from a New Science,* finds that once out of poverty, people do not get happier as they get richer, because their expectations rise at the same rate as their incomes.[93] A three-day Positive Psychology Summit was a sellout in Washington, DC, in October 2006, with 425 attending. The same fall, Harvard associate professor Tal Ben-Shahar's course "Positive Psychology" (known as "Happiness 101"), enrolled 854 students, more than any other Harvard course.[94] In the "Good Work" project, Mihaly Csikszentmihalyi of Claremont Graduate University, one of three scholars on the team,

> "has handed out pagers to thousands of people who agreed to log their mood whenever prompted to do so. People were, unsurprisingly, at their happiest when eating, carousing or pottering around the garden. But some fortunate people also found deep satisfaction from losing themselves in their work... This happy state, which Mr. Csikszentmihalyi calls 'flow,' arises most often in work that stretches a person without defeating him; work that provides 'clear goals,' 'unambiguous feedback' and a 'sense of control.'" [95]

Confirming the new *cachet* of happiness research, in May 2007 the Harvard psychology professor Daniel Gilbert won the

UK's prestigious Royal Society Prize for Science Books—"[triumphing] over other strong contenders"—for *Stumbling on Happiness*, his latest, sometimes witty insight from recent work in cognitive science and psychology.[96] The new generation of neuroscientists translate our mood swings into measurements of dopamine and serotonin and oxytocin (and cortisol and norepinephrine), and track our emotions via lit-up brain nodes on MRI scans. Extraordinarily precise and powerful new technology fuels these advances in knowledge, causing a highly interesting and revealing leap forward in the human learning curve about how we function and what makes us happy and what doesn't and why.

Researchers in the new discipline of "happiness economics" bring unaccustomed cheer to the utility-gray halls of the dismal science. For a very small country, Bhutan is big in their discussions. From the *New York Times* (October 4, 2005), "A New Measure of Well-Being from a Happy Little Kingdom:"

"What is happiness? In the United States and in many other industrialized countries, it is often equated with money...

But the small Himalayan kingdom of Bhutan has been trying out a different idea.

In 1972, concerned about the problems afflicting other developing countries that focused only on economic growth, Bhutan's newly crowned leader, King Jigme Singye Wangchuck, decided to make his nation's priority not its G.D.P. but its G.N.H., or gross national happiness.

Bhutan, the king said, needed to ensure that prosperity was shared across society and that it was balanced against preserving cultural traditions, protecting the environment and maintaining a responsive government....

Around the world, a growing number of economists, social scientists, corporate leaders and bureaucrats are trying to develop measurements that take into account not just the flow of money but also access to health care, free time with family, conservation of natural resources and other noneconomic factors.

The goal ... is in part to return to a richer definition of the word happiness, more like what the signers of the

Declaration of Independence had in mind when they included 'the pursuit of happiness' as an inalienable right equal to liberty and life itself.

The founding fathers, said John Ralston Saul, a Canadian political philosopher, defined happiness as a balance of individual and community interests. 'The Enlightenment theory of happiness was an expression of public good or the public welfare, of the contentment of the people,' Mr. Saul said. And , he added, this could not be further from 'the 20th –century idea that you should smile because you're at Disneyland.' "

There are unexpected dimensions to—and findings about – well-being or happiness and human motivation. In the 1990s, a historian researching happiness in the USA found that from the 1890's until the 1990's (the period for which measurable data was available), peak happiness occurred during two specific periods: the Great Depression and World War II. [97] Perhaps—contrary to conventional wisdom—the necessity of relying on our wits, our resourcefulness and each other for survival and success directly promotes our own happiness. Optimum well-being may *require* that we exert ourselves; push ourselves to intellectual and physical limits; engage in "real" work; rise to challenges; face adversity and extremes; cope with the unexpected; join a communal effort to accomplish some mission greater than ourselves.

How about rewards—even monetary rewards: do they stimulate our enthusiasm or overcome our objections?   Not necessarily. The psychologist Barry Schwartz, a professor at Swarthmore College, cites research which shows that when you pay people for doing things they like, they come to like these activities less, and will no longer take part in them for the intrinsic satisfaction. When Swiss citizens were asked to accept a nuclear waste dump nearby, half said they would do so (because "the dumps had to go somewhere"); but when a substantial offer of cash was added as an incentive, only 25% agreed to the proposal. Schwartz reports that in New York City, the Department of Education is offering cash rewards to some students for good attendance and good exam scores, since it seems that the intrinsic rewards of learning are not working, but expresses concern over the strategy:

> "[The] plan will distract us from investigating a more pertinent set of questions: why don't children get intrinsic satisfaction from learning in school, and how can this failing of education be fixed? Virtually all kindergartners are eager to learn. But by fourth grade, many students need to be bribed. What makes our schools so dystopian that they produce this powerful transformation, almost overnight?"[98]

Many of the core premises of traditional economics are taking fire lately, as we come to question more rigorously what *does* cause us to behave as we do. We are starting to weigh the role of "uneconomic" values in our real life—"goods" such as choice, justice, stability, diversity and other intangibles, goods which in many societies are "very scarce indeed, and highly valued," in the observation of Christopher and Miranda Meyer. "South Africans can feel the intangible return on their investment in Truth and Reconciliation, even if economists value only the costs. People vote because they feel that democracy plays a role in delivering these 'uneconomic' values."[99]

Perhaps in modern times our self-consciously happiness-oriented culture has worked perversely against our own best interest. In the successful pursuit of comfort and convenience, we may be depriving ourselves of the work and challenges which provide the most *real* satisfaction. We cannot know it, because we are not accustomed to exerting ourselves to overcome real hardship or deprivation (seldom having the need to do so). To the contrary, we go to extremes to *avoid* exerting ourselves. This paradox may explain the huge success of the "law and order" and "survival" TV programs: a backlash against too much safety and comfort; a surrogate for the predicaments and danger we rarely face, and the quick wits and strength and endurance which we seldom have need to muster in real life (except in certain high-risk or physically demanding occupations or pursuits). Has our preoccupation with comfort and convenience and leisure turned us into a culture of wimps? Timid about danger, whining at hardship, feeling entitled to be cared for and served by our government, our insurer, our litigator, our bistro server, our landscaper, our Merry Maid?

It goes without saying that not all happiness is equal. But perhaps a simple measure is how much pleasure it gives us in retrospect. As a young man, the future Supreme Court Justice Oliver Wendell Holmes, Jr. would stay overnight, after a dinner party, at the home of his fiancée Fannie Dixwell. In the morning her father, "walking briskly into the breakfast room ... would ...beam at the company through his spectacles, and remark heartily, 'Well! Did the evening's enjoyment bear the morning's reflection?'"[100]

What is "Good " ?

The discussion below is a practical look at ethics, not a learned treatise: an attempt, from a secular view, to address the complex issue of goodness and badness.

Implicit in the idea of "advancing well-being" is the assumption that life (and the state of the universe) is not a zero-sum game: that a gain for some individuals is not necessarily a loss for others; that the greater good of the human species is not necessarily offset by a loss for the planet, or vice versa. Existence, as we experience it and analyze it, certainly seems to be anything but zero-sum. On one hand, it can accumulate incalculable diversity and complexity and thrivingness, as individuals and societies and civilizations and meteorological conditions progress or improve. On the other hand, it can be tarnished or diminished or partially extinguished or eliminated altogether by an epidemic of rudeness, a tsunami, a plague, a violent clash of societies, an excess of hydrocarbons in the atmosphere, or a giant meteor strike. We believe we can take part in expanding the sum total and in improving the product. Meanwhile, we recognize that "improvement" itself can be hard to quantify. We rely on our best-yet measures of *detriment* and *benefit*, measures we calibrate using the accumulation of all earlier generations' knowledge and observation and experience, as filtered through our own knowledge, observation, and experience. In the Be-ist view of existence, there is no *absolute* good or bad, no Good and Evil. There is just the world as we observe and experience it, alone and as a group, from our singular vantage point as human beings. There is just our own (individual and communal) judgment of what we *deem* good or bad, helpful or harmful, to us or to others. We measure ourselves against our latest "best guess" benchmarks for good conduct: standards arrived at by us individually, and by a convergence of individual judgments merging in a communal consensus. We continue to try to fine-tune and reach agreement on "the rules."

Free of the constraint of testing ourselves against a pre-existing doctrine—from a religion or an ideology, for example—we can see a direct correlation between how well we behave (individually and communally) and how well we do (individually and communally). Removing from the equation things obviously beyond our control, if we behave *well* (that is, so as to cause net benefit to ourselves and the community), we by definition do well; if we behave *badly* (that is, so as to cause net harm to ourselves and the community), we by definition do badly. The incentives and disincentives are obvious to everyone. We evaluate each other's struggles and successes and failures openly as we go, without the involvement of any mysterious "third party" (and all the associated rules and go-betweens) to complicate the formula.

So there is a strong, clear *moral imperative* in Be-ism – arguably more straightforward and transparent than any to be found in pre-established doctrine. The benefits and detriments of our conduct are judged by us and our fellows every step of the way. There are judges everywhere, all the time. Not least among them sits our own inner jurist, continuously telling us right from wrong, undercutting all our rationalizations and excuses. Taken together, they constitute a powerful moral "bench," presided over by our own conscience and a jury of our peers. (When a member of the community lacks the "inner jurist"—is unable to distinguish or care about the difference between harm and benefit, has no conscience—the rest of us must take special care to safeguard that person's safety, and our own.)

Science Takes On Morality and Altruism

Morality and ethics and their origins are hot topics in a recent popular debate over the role of morality and religion in forming human societies, human values and human institutions. Neuroscientists, evolutionary biologists and psychologists, primatologists and ethnologists push ahead in their research, testing new hypotheses and making new discoveries "as we speak." The leaders in this ambitious inquiry—among them, the late William D. Hamilton, David Sloan Wilson, Frans de Waal, Marc Hauser and Daniel Goleman—have spearheaded an intensive campaign to find better empirical explanations for human morality, with new attention to the study of altruism (unselfish concern for the welfare of others). There is many a mile to go before we have a conclusive understanding of human motivations: where they come from, and how they best could be adapted to serve our well-being in the world today. But like the quest for knowledge and competency, and the need for physical action, altruism appears to be innate in us: it arises from our genes as well as our culture.

Scientists and philosophers have long been fascinated by altruistic behavior in humans, and also in chimpanzees and other non-human primates: intentional behavior which seems to benefit the group at a cost to the altruist. There always has been controversy on the subject: is altruism driven by ultimately selfish (or at least self-serving) motives, either because it rewards the giver with warm emotions (Hume), or because it induces others to cooperate with us (Robert Trivers' mathematical calculations of "reciprocal altruism")? In June 2007, University of Oregon researchers Ulrich Mayr, William Harbaugh and Daniel Burghart announced startling new evidence that yes, we *are* capable of real altruism. *New York Times* writer John Tierney reports that when the subjects of the research anonymously donated money to a local food bank, an MRI showed heightened activity in the "pleasure centers" of their brain. Interestingly, about half the subjects showed a "warm glow" response and the other half—the "egoists"—did not. The altruist impulse apparently is not *universal*. (Surprise surprise....) On the other hand, perhaps the *purest* altruism was expressed by two of the "egoists," who chose to give money to the food bank, but in doing so, did *not* register a glow in their "pleasure centers."[101]

Dutch-born psychologist, ethologist and primatologist Frans de Waal studies apes and monkeys, mostly captive troupes. The science writer Jonathan Weiner, in a *Scientific American* review of de Waal's 2006 book *Primates and Philosophers: How Morality Evolved*, reports,

> "He has documented tens of thousands of instances of chimpanzee behavior that ...we would call Machiavellian and about as many moments that we would call altruistic, even noble." De Waal argues that "[s]ympathy, empathy, right and wrong are feelings that we share with other animals; even the best part of human nature, the part that cares about ethics and justice, is also part of nature." His work refutes the view that "human morality is a thin crust on a churning urn of boiling funk...."
>
> "In reality, de Waal reminds us, dogs are social, wolves are social, chimps and macaques are social, and we ourselves are 'social to the core.' Goodness, generosity and genuine kindness come just as naturally to us as meaner feelings. We didn't have to invent compassion. When our ancestors began writing down the first codes of conduct, precepts, laws and commandments, they were elaborating on feelings that evolved thousands or even millions of years before they were born. 'Instead of empathy being an endpoint,' de Waal writes, 'it may have been the starting point.'" [102]

DeWaal uses the metaphor of a Russian doll (the smaller dolls nesting inside the larger) to explain his view of an "evolved" morality, with all its more recent developments building upon the underlying earlier ones found in ever-more-remote human ancestors.

In *Primates and Philosophers,* de Waal presents his own findings, but also includes critiques by four other contemporary evolutionary ethicists—Robert Wright, Christine Korsgaard, Philip Kitcher and Peter Singer—whose views demonstrate that the field is alive with ferment and informed argument as we try to home in on the true origins and evolution of our humanity. Their lively debate draws on the newest bioscience, but also brings back into the discussion the Swedish Finn Edward Westermarck, Charles Darwin, and some of the 18th century Enlightenment idea-masters: the Scotsmen David Hume and Adam Smith (arguing that our moral sense is rooted in our sociable emotions), and the German philosopher Immanuel Kant (making the opposing case for "reason" as the basis for morality). Altogether, de Waal's book is a provocative foray into "the latest" on how our human sense of right and wrong, good and bad, has evolved into the very *concept* of morality, with all its difficulties and challenging implications.[103]

In another contemporary take on morality, the evolutionary psychologist Marc Hauser discusses his 2006 book, *Moral Minds*:

"At the core of the book is a radical rethinking of our ideas on morality, which is based on the analogy to language, supported by an explosion of recent scientific evidence. Our moral instincts are immune to the explicitly articulated commandments handed down by religions and governments. Sometimes our moral intuitions will converge with those that culture spells out, and sometimes they will diverge...."[104]

Hauser's evidence leads him to propose that

"[A]ll humans are endowed with a *moral faculty*—a capacity that enables each individual to unconsciously and automatically evaluate a limitless variety of actions in terms of principles that dictate what is permissible, obligatory, or forbidden."[105]

"What has allowed us to live in large groups of unrelated individuals that often come and go is an evolved faculty of the mind that generates universal and unconscious judgments concerning justice and harm. Over historical time, we have invented legal policies and religions doctrine that sometimes enforce these intuitions, but often conflict with them." [106]

Altruism works in our own interest through both direct personal benefits (the pleasure of helping, the approval of others), and the many obvious advantages to us of living in a society where helpful reciprocity is expected and practiced. All the research aside, in the everyday real world we tend to proceed on the general premise that to be helpful to others is personally satisfying and also benefits the greater community.

Of course there are subsets of our fellow travelers (sometimes including us) who do not always or ever experience this motivation: who actually do not feel the inclination to make the world a better place. To single out a few:
1. Those who think the world is entirely OK as is (or "close enough");
2. Those who think the world is a "lost cause," a hopeless case, and it is futile to try to change it;
3. Those who are far too busy just trying to survive to even "go there;"
4. Those who are too preoccupied with the (hypothetical) "next world" to concern themselves with this one; or
5. Those who actually wish the world *ill*: who prefer the idea of its decline and demise (preferably in a large fireball).

We each may vacillate among the subgroups, depending on whether we just got fired from our job that morning (subset 5), or whether our beloved just revealed that she/he "loves us back" (subset 1). But by and large we tend to fall generally into that other group, "the rest of us": the ones who muddle along (or hustle along) doing good deeds for our neighbors and our communities and our good causes, regardless of the attitude of our comrades in the subsets.

There is a long current-reading list on the subject of the origins and explanation of human morality, in this fast-evolving field of science and philosophy. We would do well to stay tuned. Because it's "all about us."

Be-ism and Morality

How does a Be-ist view "morality" and "ethics"? Perhaps by proposing a different term—for example, "civil" conduct: conduct agreed upon by current consensus of the community as being on balance helpful rather than harmful, to ourselves and others, in both our personal dealings and any other domain in which we act. In this version, a consensus continues to evolve, as our culture evolves, as to what constitutes "civil" behavior. We try harder to minimize the lag between old practice and current thinking. At the same time, the community commits to a continuing effort to understand, and learn how to prevent or manage, detrimental ("uncivil") behavior, and to apply this knowledge to the best of our ability.

For the Be-ist, "civil" conduct might be defined as that which, in the judgment of an impartial observer, contributes on balance to the well-being of the individual and society. "Uncivil" conduct would be that which, in the eyes of an impartial observer, is detrimental, on balance, to the well-being of the individual and society. (Knowing the difficulty of finding a truly impartial observer, and of weighing the interest of the individual against that of society, we just make our best attempt at impartiality and fairness: this is the domain of reason and Law.) [107] Civil conduct tends to elevate our positive feelings, and reassures us and others. Uncivil conduct tends to elicit, in us and in others, feelings of shame or guilt, disgust or anger, fear or insecurity. If we act with a positive *intention*—without knowing for certain whether the outcome will succeed—we can evaluate our success in terms of our comfort with the result. If after reflection on the outcome, we find ourselves "comfortable," we probably decided "correctly." If not, we probably calculated wrong. As long as we are open to learning, our ever-accumulating experience gradually teaches us how to achieve more positive outcomes. And positive behavior (like negative behavior) is contagious; but unlike negative behavior, perhaps it generally aligns with our "default" desire to do well in life, and our (all things being equal) underlying attitude of good will towards ourselves, others and the world.

In trying for a positive view, and attempting to make good ethical or civil decisions, often the choices are not clear. The consequences of action or inaction are hard to predict. In supporting a worthy cause "beyond ourselves"—for example, the welfare of new immigrants—what if our action compromises the welfare of equally worthy people—existing working-class communities? All we can do is use intelligently the information and resources at our disposal, weigh the options accordingly, and then act (or refrain from action). As a human society, evolving over many thousands of years, we have achieved some quite extraordinary success in developing norms of civil value and behavior ("civilization"). We continue to strive for a higher level of civility. We may not be idealistic about the *perfectability* of ourselves or the world, but based on progress so far, are we not justified in a *hopefulness* that we can continue to *do better*?

Badness

The 2006 Man Booker prizewinning novelist Kiran Desai, speaking about her bestselling book *The Inheritance of Loss* – a rich, ironical and rather dark novel of immigration and class in Himalayan India and New York City—explains, "...[A]s a writer I am trying to understand hate and anger." [108]

The obvious human obstacle to good and advancement in the world, the opposing force which stymies and thwarts us all along the way, is the existence—in us and around us—of "badness." Disturbing and terrible and tragic things happen all the time, caused intentionally by us and our fellows, or allowed to happen as we stand by. We are notoriously curious about the bad: the deviant, the perverse, the taboo, the malicious, the unfortunate, the tragic. We scoop up the gory details of the latest mayhem or tragedy or cataclysm—global or local—from the newspapers, the magazines, the radio, TV, the internet. The "real" bad news isn't enough. We flock to the movies, become slave to the TV programs and video games, devour the bestsellers that dish out excess and violence and brutality—every sort of damage imaginable. (Note the huge following of the TV series "24" or "CSI" or "Fear Factor.") We feel the pull of the "dark side:" the risk, the danger, the drama. *The New York Times* columnist Bob Herbert, on the anniversary of the death of Martin Luther King, observes, "We've honored Dr. King, but we've never listened to him. Our addiction to the joy of violence is far too strong." [109] We experience a (somewhat appalled, sometimes addictive) fascination with stories of treachery, malice, sadism, masochism, sociopathy. Stephen King and Anne Rice and (for the more high-brow) Joyce Carol Oates rule the fiction best-seller lists with tales of psychopathy and the macabre, rife with gratuitous mayhem. The pre-adolescent thrill of self-fright carries over into adulthood with hugely popular films such as *The Exorcist* and *Silence of the Lambs* and its sequel *Hannibal Rising*. Popular culture takes as its icons beautiful prostitutes ("Pretty Woman") and "badass" gangsters and thugs, and racquet-hurling tennis champions.

In March 2006, a Henri de Toulouse Lautrec exhibition—paintings and drawings romanticizing the absinthe bars and brothels of *fin de siecle* Paris—opened at the National Gallery in Washington, DC, to the second largest opening crowd in its history (after the opening exhibit of the "Mona Lisa" in 1963). In 2004, *Reading Lolita in Tehran,* an account by the Iranian professor Azar Nifisi of teaching Western literature "underground" to young women in Tehran in 1995, was enshrined on the *New York Times* bestseller list for twenty-one weeks. (Would a book titled *"Reading Jane Eyre in Tehran"* –another of the books she taught—have found the same audience?) The graphic depiction of extreme sexuality—especially illicit sex—sells in all venues. It is the most popular product by far in the prodigious open market of the internet. Apparently (so far), even when widely available and easily accessible, it feeds a universal and insatiable appetite. Crudeness, harsh satire, ugly parody, vitriol and obscenity rule on the "comedy" circuit and on much of talk radio. "Bad" is the new "good" (or maybe not so new).

On the under side of bad behavior lurks the "tyranny of sunk costs": the burning of bridges which makes it hard to get back to the high road once we jump or fall off the straight and narrow. It is a high and long-term price for an impulsive escapade or a momentary succumbing to temptation, a price paid by the perpetrator as well as the victim. A rational society, which relies for health and survival on the cooperation of its members, understandably finds it difficult to forgive damage, especially intentional damage, inflicted on the community. Even harm caused by inadvertence or carelessness or a momentary wild impulse raises doubt as to our trustworthiness, and creates a pothole for us in the road ahead.

How many of us, living in relative prosperity, remain vulnerable to the curious allure of badness, and why? Usually we do side with the "good guy" of the film or the novel or the play. But we do seem to love the mayhem. We like our heroes and heroines downtrodden and disaffected and horribly aggrieved — overcoming insurmountable odds to consign the vicious and powerful villain to oblivion. Given all our other options, we choose to use a free Saturday night—and pay $20—to see *that* movie. We perceive the violent story as an entertainment. Is it just an antidote to a relatively safe and tame life: the test of wits, the cleverness and nerve and agility of the hero and the villain; the danger and suspense, excitement and mischief and din?

The cause of our fascination with—the strong appeal of—bad behavior, and our occasional compulsion to try it out, is not necessarily well understood. In these times, is it a rebellious holdover from the social turmoil, assertiveness, and combativeness of the 1960's and 70's—the civil rights movement, the feminist movement, the Vietnam conflict—when Americans, and the West in general, felt increasingly betrayed by the "the Establishment," the core institutions whose authority formerly had been accepted and respected? Or is it maybe a more deep-seated need to understand and come to terms with, even succumb to, the innate dark side of our nature: negative impulses, forbidden passions, secret demons, illicit desires (those which we know would cause damage or pain to ourselves or others if acted upon)?

In March 2006, PBS aired a bio-documentary on the playwright Eugene O'Neil (1888-1953), with commentary by the contemporary playwright Tony Kushner. Kushner explained how O'Neil (*The Iceman Cometh* and *Moon for the Misbegotten*) brought a revolution to American theater by exposing boldly, on stage, troubling new dimensions of the human psyche—raw new dramas about the human struggle for purpose and belonging. The effect on the actors, as well as the audience, was "transcendent" and "profound." The expression of emotional truth, no matter how dark, left them deeply moved. We respond powerfully to the truth about ourselves even when it is dark and not bright. We find the real truth "clean" if not always "pretty." In explaining us to ourselves, it purges us, bonds us to each other ("for worse" as well as for better), and in its way, sets us free.

So we are, and always have been, attracted to and moved by dramas of humankind struggling with the temptation or the will toward harm and destruction. We still wrestle with how and whether human damage can be justified, or avenged, or forgiven. We mount yet another production of *Oedipus* or *Macbeth,* and the theater is still full. As we like our comedy, so we like our tragedy.

Sin

What is the link between badness and "sin"? Could it be argued that "sin," a concept originating with religion, raises badness to greater prestige? Do religious strictures have the perverse side effect of giving "sin" a *cachet*—an alluring wickedness, to be excused and forgiven because it shows we are "only human," and carries with it the juicy extra promise, the drama and glory and catharsis of *redemption*? "Without sin there is no redemption"— a powerful and intriguing concept. Almost a "call" to sin—for the glory of "repentance." In this respect, does religion actually dramatize, romanticize and create license for bad conduct? What if we tried calling "sin" what it really is: behavior which deliberately, by commission or omission, *inflicts harm.* Sin causes harm. Sin does damage. Much "sin," such as murder or theft or adultery, causes personal or civil hurt. (Some "sin" undermines religion, but causes no civil harm.) Faced frontally, perhaps "sin"—the sort that causes *real* harm—would seem less romantic, less dramatic (or melodramatic) and less innocent. We might take a more sober and less tolerant view of those (ourselves sometimes included) who inflict damage on others. Holding a more hard-headed view of "sin," perhaps we could become more intelligent and effective in preventing damage – in restraining ourselves and others from doing harm, in protecting ourselves from and rehabilitating the transgressors.

We might revisit, too, the conventional wisdom that "we have to learn from our own mistakes"—that somehow we are not only expected, but entitled, to experiment with behavior that *is already known* to be dangerous and destructive, behavior which not infrequently results in serious or lifelong damage to ourselves or others: binge drinking, hard drugs, promiscuous sex, wild driving, cheating, gratuitous rudeness, and even criminal acts (shoplifting, stealing cars or other people's possessions). We boast about our wild youth. But how does the boast look in the context of the harm and the damage: the actual toll of bad acts; the pain to the victims of our bad behavior (family members, community); the unreasonable risks taken which easily could have caused real tragedy? At what point does the *benefit* from "wildness"—learning from mistakes, taking risks which result in rewards—no longer justify the damage caused or the risks taken? As a "rational" society, to what extent do we believe that each of us, in order to learn the rules of moral and civil conduct, must break them first?

Is it even possible that we have come to think—either singly or as a community—that civil conduct, good manners, are unimportant or even objectionable? If so, why? (What is *detrimental* about civil behavior, and *desirable* about uncivil behavior?) "What is going on here" probably could withstand more scrutiny. Meanwhile, contradictions in our current thinking will continue to humble us in the search for solutions to making human society more cooperative in its actions and more cheerful in its demeanor.

Misery

Of course the other side of the coin from *well-being* (the goods commonly valued by all) is *misery*, in its many shapes and degrees: the *detriments* deplored by all—the opposites to, or absence of, the requirements for well-being. Any analysis of well-being and how to achieve it must recognize and face "the enemy": the underlying causes of misery and unhappiness; how to reduce and eliminate them; and meanwhile, how to mitigate the damage. Throughout history, we have wrestled with the seemingly intractable problems faced by humankind: physical and mental injury and disease and impairment; natural catastrophes; violence against each other, against other species, and against the planet itself; out-of-control greed; lust for power; domination of the weak by the strong; fanaticism; bigotry; bad-faith dealing; gross indulgence of physical appetites; destructive addiction to harmful substances and/or behaviors; carelessness and neglect. The damage wreaks havoc on the lives of victims of natural calamities such as earthquake, drought, fire, flood, and epidemic; or victims of human calamities such as war, domestic abuse, accident or genetic infirmity. The heavy toll on humanity is physical, emotional and intellectual, social, economic and cultural.

A most troubling challenge in combating human misery is learning how to cope with *disaffection* in our fellows: with the individuals or subgroups among us who lack empathy and sympathy toward their own species, or in the extreme, who bear us ill will and are intent on doing us harm. We need to discover how to prevent sociopathy and psychopathy from developing; how to treat the sufferers (if possible) to restore their empathy and good will; and meanwhile, how to protect ourselves from the disaffected.

We need to learn more about the mechanisms which induce those who have inflicted harm to do so again: how to reverse the destructive pattern of damage and bring the aggressors back into society. (In South Africa and Sarajevo and Northern Ireland, groundbreaking work has been done in this area through initiatives such as South Africa's Truth and Reconciliation Commission, rehabilitating aggressors who have taken part in sectarian violence, through a process of apology, reparation and forgiveness.)

Our experience seems to show that ideology and religious zealotry can inspire violence and aggression which in themselves become addictive: the thrill, the adrenalin rush, the "high" of violence becomes confused with the mission (itself perhaps worthy) of a movement or a religion. Abused or neglected minority communities suddenly swing into action—for good reason—against their aggressors or governments. Africa becomes a battlefield of tribe against tribe, fighting for territory and a decent life and respect, causing a new generation of Africans to become corrupted and hardened and damaged by the continuing violence. We read daily about the havoc wrought by urban gangs of young marauding males (sometimes females too, as participants or hangers-on), even in "advanced" societies such as the USA. They constitute an insidious social threat, an expression of the grave danger that looms when law and order are not operational or respected, and when legitimate social, economic and political grievances have no effective means of redress.

Equally pressing is the challenge to restore the trust and sympathy of the victims of violence: to "turn around" victims as well as perpetrators so they can resume a positive life among us. Perhaps neuroscience and behavioral science and economics and political science eventually will discover better solutions to these entrenched human problems, which otherwise seem to perpetuate themselves indefinitely and will continue to poison the bloodstream of society until they are solved. Much of the work of advancing our well-being must include, by definition, reducing (and eventually eliminating) the causes of misery.

But in our efforts to overcome human trouble, it may be helpful to think of human despair—often a consequence of the dark side of the real human psyche—as the reverse manifestation of an overwhelming love of life, but coupled with a profound inability to cope with it. As social scientists and economists have gravitated recently to the study of positive psychology and "happiness economics," perhaps they could embark on a mirror study of "misery psychology" and "misery economics": a well-documented misery index (perhaps a better gauge of well-being than a poverty index), so that we learn more accurately the extent and nature of the challenge. To define our problems more clearly, in order to combat them more effectively, we need cultural and psychological measures of well-being and of misery, as well as economic measures.

* * *

The Practice: Pursuing Well-being

Once we home in on a general definition of well-being, and agree that advancing the well-being of our fellows (as well as ourselves) is a worthy mission, what next? Perhaps we start with very basic things.

First, be nice.

"We have a great deal more kindness than is ever spoken."
-- Emerson, "Friendship"

It seems like the simplest possible requirement: to be civil and considerate (even affectionate) toward family members, workplace colleagues, whomever we encounter on a given day. Yet so often, "being nice" requires an unexpected degree of self-control: *consciously refraining* from a negative or impatient or critical comment. Forbearance does not come easily—softening the edge of our voice and our demeanor. But the payoff is large. Disciplining ourselves to be *agreeable* (rather than disagreeable or indifferent) makes a huge difference in the chemistry of the family or the workplace or any other setting. Civility affects directly, if sometimes subtly, the well-being of every person in the group. It can be so simple—for example, greeting family members or co-workers with "Good morning" every day: an almost effortless formality, but one which starts the day well.

Elinor Ochs, a linguistic anthropologist and MacArthur Fellow, leads a large team of scientists at UCLA in a study of the modern family:

> "In the observed families, wives stop what they are doing and welcome home a returning spouse only a little more than a third of the time. Mostly, they are too irritable or busy to do so, says Ochs. Husbands do better, with more than half offering a positive greeting to a spouse. Children greet their fathers ... positively only a third of the time, and often don't even look up when the dad reenters the house.
>
> 'I ask myself, is it no longer the case that we're supposed to appreciate our parents or our spouse? Is it a relic of the Victorian family? I don't think so,' says Ochs, who partly attributes the change to the rise of what she terms a 'child-dominated' society that denigrates parental respect."[110]

Good behavior and good manners are powerful. They indicate self-mastery and good will—civilization. Their absence suggests the opposite. Screaming and yelling and ranting may be okay, but only to alert someone to extreme danger or injustice. Overused, they soon lose their efficacy, and worse, they erode good feeling in the community. Crankiness and edginess are uncivil. If we can't be kind, curb our negativity, cut each other a little slack, how can we expect to enjoy a civil society?

Second, we predispose ourselves to be useful and helpful in our daily life, aided by an understanding of how our particular abilities suit us to certain kinds of usefulness. We agree to suffer a little inconvenience or make at least a minimal effort on behalf of others in the normal course of the day. We take reasonable action to protect the safety of and prevent harm to those around us. If we are able and so choose, we exert ourselves more, and "put ourselves out" to coach a child's soccer team, or drive for "Meals on

Wheels," or volunteer at the Red Cross blood bank, or tutor a student with disabilities.

Third, we develop and hone our own abilities in our chosen field(s) to serve some greater good, through the product(s) of our work and the manner in which we carry out the work. We act collaboratively, in the interest of improving our product. We help others achieve proficiency, where we are able. We are generous with our expertise and knowledge and encouragement. There are always tradeoffs, of course, and difficult decisions as to whose well-being to support, at the expense of someone else or some other group. For instance, Roland Fryer, the Harvard economist, grapples with the tradeoffs between investing in success in a cultural subgroup versus investing in success in "larger society." [III] Everyday life is full of hard choices without absolute answers.

Fourth, we focus our vocation or avocation on a field where the "product" specifically advances the well-being of others: medicine, health, education, social services, or public policy. We choose a stint, or a full career, in public service.

In September 2007, *Time* magazine featured a major story, "A Time to Serve," which proposed a plan for voluntary national service in the USA. The plan listed ten ideas:
1. **Create a (Federal) National-Service Baby Bond** for each baby born, to be used (like the GI Bill) if the person performs at least one year of national or military service.
2. **Make National Service a Cabinet-Level Department**
3. **Expand Existing Programs like AmeriCorps and the National Senior Volunteer Corps**
4. **Create an Education Corps**
5. **Institute a Summer of Service**
6. **Build a Health Corps**
7. **Launch a Green Corps**
8. **Recruit a Rapid-Response Resource Corps**
9. **Start a National-Service Academy**
10. **Create a Baby-Boomer Education Bond** (for older

volunteers' children or grandchildren or a student they designate)[112]

In the same issue of *Time*, Caroline Kennedy extolled the continuing contributions of Peace Corps volunteers, who return to the U.S. as teachers, "bringing the lessons they learned to the kids who need them most."[113]

With an extreme commitment to the common good, we exert ourselves to the max and break vital new ground in areas that will enhance the well-being of our fellows: a new drug to combat or prevent disease; a ground-breaking new policy to cure social or behavioral ills such as domestic violence or drug abuse.

Fifth, we improve the aesthetics and functionality and environmental friendliness of our human-made world: our buildings, roads, parks, water and wastewater systems, utilities; our developed landscapes, whether urban, suburban, or rural. Usually we live and work in a largely human-designed-and-built environment. To the extent we can afford it (economically and otherwise), we choose a physical environment in which we feel comfortable and productive—one which suits our own interests and preferences and temperament. Once settled, we become "alert" inhabitants of our place, paying attention to flaws in the local environment and taking the initiative (or working with others) to mitigate or correct them.

Would we do well to think harder about the impact on us, from childhood onward, of our physical surroundings: our homes; our schools; our public and commercial buildings; our institutions; our roads and bridges and airports and railroads? Does it matter what sort of buildings and spaces we inhabit? If so, why and how much? In dense human settlements, what is the effect on us, or our less fortunate fellows, of life in a highrise apartment block? How does that compare as a living environment, especially for the under-advantaged, with the vast lateral (as opposed to vertical) sprawl of urban slums or the sun-blasted refugee camps of Kenya? How about the effect of school buildings and their surroundings on our children, who spend a large part of their first twenty-one years of life in school? Do we pay adequate attention to this issue, let alone address it seriously?

Malcolm Gladwell, in his best-selling book *The Tipping Point*, talks about the Power of Context in our lives: how "we are more than sensitive to changes in context. We're exquisitely sensitive to them."[114] Although he focuses on the example of the Broken Windows theory of criminal behavior—that if a broken window is left unrepaired more windows will be broken—his point is that the smallest change in the physical environment (as well as the social environment) can "tip" people towards better or worse behavior.[115] Gladwell cites the findings of psychologist Judith Harris (*The Nurture Assumption*) that "peer influence and community influence are more important than family influence in determining how children turn out."[116] The reason is that "children are powerfully shaped by their external environment." If, as Gladwell concludes, "it is possible to be a better person on a clean street or in a clean subway than in one littered with trash and graffiti," how about the possibilities on the *upside*? The good that could come from an *especially* beautiful and human-inspiring built environment? The buildings of our lives may exert a far more subtle and formative influence on us and our societies than has yet been recognized. Would we "do better" to spend our lifetime in a built environment that is beautiful and uplifting as well as functional and economic and efficient—one that is designed and built for the best use and highest enjoyment of us, the users? (What *is* it about Paris?)

In 2006 the Swiss writer Alain de Botton published a fresh new study of architecture, *The Architecture of Happiness,* showing how buildings embody a message and a set of values. The architectural critic Robert Campbell quotes from de Botton and adds commentary of his own:

" 'Buildings *speak*. They speak of democracy or aristocracy, openness or arrogance, welcome or threat, a sympathy for the future or a hankering for the past.' He could have added more such words. Buildings speak of risk-taking or cowardice, of individualism or conformity, of nature or artifice, of wealth or

poverty, of handicraft or machinery, of the local or the global, of representation or abstraction, of permanence or change....
We admire the buildings that speak to our values—or, at least, the values we wish other people to perceive in us." [117]

If our architecture and design and built environment are influencing our lives significantly, who can represent us effectively to ensure that we perform better on the "design and build" front— for our children if not for ourselves?

Back to the "how-to" list for well-being:

Sixth, we give financial support, or in-kind contributions, or promotion and "pitching" to endeavors that advance well-being, or to individuals who are in need or who work on behalf of others in need. We also give them our political support and our vote.

Countless acts of personal or civic generosity—millions— occur every day, most of them unremarked except by those directly involved. As one among the millions: April 2005, in a small town in Massachusetts, a couple struggle to care for their 5-year-old son who has a progressive degenerative muscular disease and is confined to a small motorized wheelchair. His mother is recovering from a recurrence of breast cancer, and the dad is maxed out, financially and emotionally, supporting his family and helping care for the ill son and two other children. Into this situation come a couple of neighbors: they persuade the TV show "Extreme Makeover" to take on a complete rebuilding of the family's house to make it accessible to the child. The entire tradesforce of the town—rival electricians and masons, carpenters and plumbers, roofers and painters—show up and get to work, collaborating for the first time ever, volunteering their tools and labor to carry out the project, often working nights and weekends. Moms all over town hold bake sales and parties and special events to raise funds for building materials and interior furnishings. Learning that the boy is an avid Red Sox fan, old adversaries among the local landscaping contractors converge to transform the back yard, creating an entrancing mini-version of Fenway Park, complete with "Green Monster" back wall and scoreboard, and a paved run around the bases. There is great hoopla when the TV producers and host show up, but long after they are gone—a year or more later—the townspeople still are pitching in to help out. The community takes itself by surprise: it did not know it could do such a thing.

Seventh, we share our own access to the "goods" of life with others: to beautiful and interesting places; to recreational, athletic and social activities; to good books and articles and media programs; to cultural events (music, film, art, dance, theater, lectures, fashion and design shows); to fine cuisine or burgers in the back yard; or to the "bazaar" (or the mall), for the double pleasure of "gathering" together.

The seven points above are a sample starter list for the "advancing human well-being" mission. The list has an infinite number of possible forms and points, and an infinite number of applications, but as they say, you have to start somewhere. Paraphrasing Emerson, as he spoke to the mechanics and apprentices of Boston in 1841 in a lecture on "Man the Reformer," we can do good—and at the same time pursue happiness—by striving **to be, in our place, a free and helpful person.**

Doing Better

When society forms a common view of good and bad, we establish norms and practical means (legal systems, social *mores*) of working toward the good and away from the bad. We agree to work aggressively against detrimental activity, and to teach and encourage beneficial activity. We generally accept that this is the responsibility of each member of the society, and of all the groups within the society. We strive to learn what it is that helps—what works—and we mark progress on many fronts all the time. Practitioners out in the world, such as the social entrepreneurship leader Bill Drayton (founder of the influential citizen-sector group

Ashoka), and scientists in the lab, such as the social neuroscientist Daniel Goleman, intrepidly advance the frontier of doing-better. [118]

Still, it is not easy weigh the beneficial versus detrimental effects of everything we do. Usually the tension is between the interest of an individual (who is competing as well as cooperating with others), and society's interest in creating an orderly community which fulfills optimally the needs and wants of *all* its members. And then, of course, there are the multiple competing interests among communities, everywhere and at every scale. New behavioral research suggests that communities in which cooperation is the norm probably win in the long run; therefore, the individuals in a "prosocial" group ultimately benefit from their group's ethic of cooperation. (The evolutionary biologist David Sloan Wilson finds that, although selfish behavior can be an advantage within groups, prosocial groups beat selfish groups—not only for humans but for all creatures.) [119] But our fate as a global society certainly depends upon our reaching a clearer understanding of the dynamics of group interests, and how to avoid or resolve conflicts among competing groups.

Even when a new idea goes counter to the prevailing wisdom or the cultural norms, we need to be open-minded to the full spectrum of "what might work." Is there a possibility, for example, that a more enlightened secularity will see the emergence of a more conservative code of behavior: a moderating of the modern trend toward ever more liberal extremes of self-expression and individual self-assertion; a growing interest in commonality and concern for the well-being of the community, even at some cost to our individuality? In a fast-globalizing age, where human societies are ever more closely linked and interdependent, such a macro trend would not be unexpected, and may already be under way.

Often the inherent complexity of a particular situation stymies or foils us in our attempt to do the right thing. We Westerners deplore in the extreme the torment and slaughter of rural villagers in Darfur, Sudan. But even although everything occurring there affronts our entire system of shared human values, we see no *clear* way to stop the carnage, because the external and internal political situation of Sudan is so extremely complicated. Our only good option is to persist, to try harder to discover and implement a solution—and to listen widely for good suggestions from elsewhere.

Service

At his inaugural address in 1961, President John F. Kennedy rallied a young generation to national and international service. He laid down the gauntlet with the memorable challenge: "Ask not what your country can do for you. Ask what you can do for your country." Since then 190,000 American Peace Corps volunteers (including some not so young) have launched into a two-year *work* commitment, often in primitive, highly challenging, and even hazardous conditions, in countries throughout the developing world. They perform arduous service ("the hardest job you'll ever love") under their country's flag, enlisted in the human mission of advancing liberty, justice, and dignity not only at home but in distant lands. The Peace Corps and programs like it are active on all continents of the world today, but with a profile so low as to be almost invisible. On the home front, comparable groups of volunteers have served and continue to work in impoverished urban and rural communities through domestic programs such as TeachAmerica and City Year.

Taken together, the veterans of the service programs comprise a sizeable group of citizens, largely unsung and unrecognized in their own country or even their own community, who have acquired well-earned understanding of the enormous personal rewards (as well as the frustration and sometimes anguish) of performing hard duty for a sustained period in unfamiliar and challenging territory. At the completion of their service, they return to civilian life with a modest stipend, in exchange for a priceless and productive experience which changes their life and their perspective on humanity forever.

The veteran journalist Jim Lehrer, speaking at Harvard University Commencement in June 2006, argued for "instituting compulsory national service in the United Sates, saying it would ... reconnect individuals in a society whose members are growing increasingly apart.

'I have never seen us more disconnected from each other than we are now,' Lehrer said...

Instead of coming together – people are breaking into like-minded splinter groups, economic disparities are widening, and politics are exacerbating the situation....

Lehrer himself served in the U. S. Marine Corps during peacetime, the experience throwing him together with men from a wide variety of racial, ethnic, economic and social backgrounds.

" 'In that diverse company, I learned to be responsible for others. I learned to be dependent on others. I learned there was more to life than me, me, me, me.'

[Lehrer] called for a national discussion about implementing ... compulsory service [and] didn't offer specific guidelines, but said the service could encompass the military, the Peace Corps, and other areas.

'I believe we need a new, hard, real-world dose of shared experience,' Lehrer said."[120]

What perhaps is most unrecognized about the performance of service—of hard work for a communal cause—is its positive impact on the *server*. The intensity of the experience, the bonds that it forges with fellow-workers and new acquaintances, the demand it makes on our inner resources, and the fulfillment that come from having done our part, can find no substitute in an easy or self-serving life. To expect (and exact) a year or two of service from every young adult citizen might contribute more to their adult well-being than almost any other kind of experience. A universal requirement for service could have another broad social benefit: it would level the playing field, in that *all of us* would have "paid our dues" through service of some sort, giving us a common experience, a more equal civic standing, the sense of fairness and solidarity that comes from the knowledge that we each have done our share for the communal good.

In 1997, using data from the World Values Survey, Ronald Inglehart produced a graph which suggests how human striving for well-being is playing out globally, in a "macro" sense. The graph shows that societies, originally sustained by religious and communal values under traditional authority systems, begin to modernize. Traditional communalism gives way to individual motivation (for material success and achievement), leading the society to a steep rise in economic growth, modernization, and a rational law-based structure. The peak of the graph represents the maximum material "success" and "effort" of the society. Then, representing "Postmodernization" (the "most advanced" of today's societies, such as the USA), the graph gently slopes downward toward "Postmaterialist Values," characterized by "de-emphasis of authority" and "maximizing well-being." Maximizing well-being seems, in this case, to be generally equated with "maximum self-expression," and assumes that adequate security and material well-being have been achieved.[121] So in 1997 (a decade ago), "maximum self expression" was cast as the ultimate goal of well-being (at least as framed by this global survey). The verdict is not yet in as to whether "self-expression," once achieved, actually *is* the ultimate key to human well-being.

Only time will tell if as a species we are advancing beyond the express pursuit of "self-expression" to a more communal aspiration, motivated by the realization that "we're all in it together;" that working together productively itself may produce a high degree of well-being; and that it is incumbent on us to collaborate and cooperate to ensure our continued survival, let alone happiness. It may be time for us together to raise the bar a notch—to think in terms of optimizing our own potential for the good of the world, once we have basically secured the good of ourselves. Perhaps, in modern times, we have been experiencing an *aspiration lag*—a gap between what we are being *told* to want (by the media, big business, our holdover materialistic aims) and what, if we took an honest inventory of our "best" self, we would find we *really* want. We might discover that what we really want corresponds to what we really need, as a community, if we are to survive and thrive in the long run. The evolution of our aspirations seems to be an organic process: not self conscious, but sometimes consciously manipulated by specific interests (commercial, or political, religious or other). We are "making it up as we go," but not necessarily aware of the influences behind our motivation. If we were more analytical—better students of how we and our societies are evolving—we perhaps could spare ourselves some of the agony along the way. We could become more effective in acting in our real individual and communal self interest. We make progress on this front all the time, through important new work in all the human sciences. But as with everything, we could be doing better at both the learning, and putting the learning into practice.

In sum, there seem to be at least two cultural obstacles to greater well-being in modern society. The first is our success in achieving what we *thought* was well-being: personal physical and material comfort and convenience. We may have convinced ourselves that ultimate happiness is a hot day at the beach with a cold keg. But the great beach party may linger in mind more for the sunburn and the hangover if we have not earned it first. And because we are "social animals" and must work together to achieve security and success as a society, a second obstacle may be in our occasional tendency to focus overmuch on our mission for self expression, at the expense of the welfare of the community. As always, the trick is in the balance.

Looking for Grace in a Secular Age

The great challenge to a post-religion culture is to learn how best to face—endure and overcome—grief, loss, pain, fear, bitterness, jealousy and injustice in the real world without the solace of "god." In taking on this challenge we are assisted daily by examples and exemplars from the present and the past, of our fellows who rise (or rose) to adversity with extraordinary grace and strength and humor—and with or without religion. All around us, often in quiet corners, we see indomitable courage: strong lessons from cancer patients, refugees, disaster victims, Alzheimer's sufferers and their kin, AIDS orphans, war amputees, the cruelly bereaved, who manage to rise above or endure with dignity great loss or suffering or dislocation. Do we understand (well enough) what inner resources these people call upon, and how we ourselves could learn to summon those resources? What are the special qualities, innate in us all, that can be tapped to deal with disaster or grief? How do we bring them forward when needed? In this new age, we can look freshly at old ideas, and take a keener and more practical look at "what works."

By working collegially in the common interest, homing in on new knowledge and improved analysis, we may truly have the best-ever prospects for identifying the real causes of our pain and suffering, and for finding better solutions. Because of enormous advances in medicine, science and technology, the odds of success today are more promising than ever before. The progress we have made already is owed largely to our increasing secularism: our practice of (and belief in) working in a rigorous analytical environment to investigate and explain human behavior and natural phenomena. As science-based thought continues to displace older doctrines, the prospects for success in advancing human well-being will only increase. And they will increase at a faster pace if *as a society* we clear our heads; gather our resources; focus on the real-world possibilities of making our lives better; and resume our lives with new energy and higher aspirations.

Into the Future

The modern era of "deconstruction" of our old institutions and values—beginning in earnest in the 1960's, and culminating in the punk and heavy metal and aggressive rap, the crudeness and lewdness of today's grunge subculture—may be, in effect, a productive purge of "old" culture, a destructive tumult in advance of a new age of rationality. So rather than succumb to the *agonistes*—the school of angst and dolor (a weak and passive position, although hip in *film noir* and *cinéma vérité*)—we can decide instead on a strong approach. We can recommit to tackling hard problems as solvable challenges, expecting to gain eventual success if we approach them with energy and pragmatism, using all the new tools available. And we can take heart and new resolve from the fact that huge strides forward are occurring on so many fronts, keeping pace with advances in technology and communications; with breakthroughs in the physical and biological sciences and medicine; with new understanding of anthropology and sociology and psychology; and with our increasing comprehension of the interrelatedness of all these fields—their "consilience" (in E.O. Wilson's term).

At the same time, we honor and need our past sages whose distilled experience and insight and images still have the ring of truth. From them, as well as from our contemporaries, we can glean the best kernels of wisdom about *real* life, and how to think about and cope with its dark side. Recently, at a memorial service for an American molecular biologist who had grown up in China, his son referred to a timeworn family copy of Lao Tzu's *Dao De Jing* (the "Book of Tao," 600 B.C.). The maxim he cited (in his own words), went something like this: "Our troubles are like a boulder in a mountain stream: our life flows past the obstacle and forms again and so continues."

※ ※ ※

Chapter 13

Do Better: Advance the Well-being of the Planet

For more than four billion years the Earth has been morphing into the "blue marble" we inhabit today. It has survived inconceivable physical extremes, cataclysmic forces of heat and pressure and radiation and tumult. It is a robust rock, but on and near its surface a huge network of living ecosystems survives and evolves through a delicate and dynamic interdependency which we are only beginning to understand. In the interest of our own survival, we want to sustain the balance.

As we need a working understanding of human well-being, so we need a definition of well-being for the natural world, if we are to consider intelligently how to improve its condition. We acknowledge a great debt to the contemporary scientists whose vast store of hard-won information and insight gives us the raw material for a comprehensive and refined definition. Some of the best-known among them—E. O. Wilson, Jared Diamond, Brian Greene and Daniel Goleman—have created vital new bridges from the sciences to the humanities and to the general populace through their popular writings and media discussions on the latest environmental science and its implications. With a special gift for explaining the gamut of scientific thought and discovery, from the smallest particles and organisms to the "big picture" of world ecology and the evolution of the universe, they are bringing the amazing new knowledge into our libraries and lives, "spreading the news" in this fast-expanding modern enlightenment. [122]

But here, as with the discussion of human well-being, we will begin with a common-sense "civilian" definition of well-being for the natural world.

What is Environmental Well-being?

A working definition of *well-being for the natural world* might include the following attributes, incorporating the reasonable assumption that we prefer a natural world which is hospitable to human life, as well as to the diverse other life forms; therefore, we favor the well-being of our own species over other species which would threaten it (such as the Ebola virus). The list:

1. A **climate** which, in its weather and temperature, can well sustain at least as much diversity of life and habitat as now exists, on the land and in the water.

2. **Clean air**, that is, air with a chemical composition that is healthful to existing plant and animal species.

3. **Clean water**, including surface water, groundwater, and oceans and seas, in sufficient supply, and with a chemical composition and temperature that will sustain existing plant and animal species.

4. **Arable land:** soil whose physical and biological and chemical characteristics are conducive to sustainably growing a variety and quantity of plants sufficient to feed humans and all other species.

5. A healthy **land cover** of trees, shrubs, small and microscopic plants, grasses, and aquatic plants, at least as diverse in number of species and geographic dispersion as now exists.

6. A robust population of **animal species**—including, and with some qualified preference for, humans—from the smallest life forms to the largest mammals, at least as diverse in its numbers and geographic dispersion as now exists.

7. An underlying **geological array** of rocks and soils and minerals which, if exploited of its material for human purposes, is restored to a stability and topography and freedom from toxic contaminants which make it enduringly safe for humans and local animal species, and aesthetically compatible with its geographical surroundings.

Pursuing environmental well-being

How do we approach "improvement" of the attributes listed above?

First, perhaps, by slowing or stopping the degradation of the natural environment which is occurring now, in every category above; and second, by maintaining and enhancing existing healthy environments to assure that they not only survive, but thrive.

To accomplish these ends we need to understand how plant and animal species, land, air and water function, both in themselves and with each other. Then we need to know how human behavior is harming or helping the species-land-air-water ecology. Next, we must determine how our (human) efforts can most effectively benefit rather than degrade the ecosystem. Finally, we must carry out the work.

The dual engine for all these tasks is science and technology: data-gathering, research, analysis, hypothesizing, designing, building, testing, manufacturing and applying. Already we (as a species) commit enormous resources to this task and these diverse areas of science and technology: much of "science" is by definition directly or indirectly devoted to this work. Our technology springs from science, and vice versa. The work of investigating and improving the environment (for us human beings as well as the whole ecosystem) is enmeshed in the functioning of our modern culture, not "something apart." The clean water (hot as well as cold) that comes from the tap; the drugs and medical procedures and regimens we rely on to maintain and improve our health; the tomatoes and mozzarella for the pizza, the cotton and polyester for the tee shirt, the pine planks and urethane finish for the floor (all of our food, clothing and shelter); the computer and internet technology which make possible the collection and sorting and transmission of huge amounts of data for research (as in the plant and human genome projects): all are the products of sophisticated and dogged scientific study and technological innovation by human beings like us.

Biotechnology—the technology with which we harness and examine and manipulate the natural world—seems to be leading us toward an increasingly "neo-biological" civilization. We use the principles of biology to organize our man-made world, and vice versa; distinctions between "engineered" biology and "bio"-technology start to blur.[123] Steering and energizing and funding the scientific efforts and the development and production of technology are the many players who make and implement environmental policy: governments, the citizen sector (the Sierra Club, the Nature Conservancy, local land trusts), business and industry, even individual citizens. (Some of the environmental culprits also come from such groups, their actions causing harm to the natural world because they have conflicting aims, or inadequate understanding of the consequences of their acts, or are indifferent to environmental damage.)

The list of practical ways to improve the environment is long, and—because society increasingly is concerned and knowledgeable—comparatively well publicized, at least in advanced societies. Global warming, a looming planetary issue, has brought together an enormous international confederation of scientists, and is a topic of earnest conversation at dinner tables and cafes and schoolrooms around the world. Owing to gaps in our knowledge and/or lack of consensus among the experts, sometimes the right path is not clear. In that case, we civilians must rely on our own assessment of the science to inform our action or inaction. Our responsibility is to become as well-informed as we reasonably can. The field of endeavor is so very broad—improving the "natural world"—that a token list of practices is all that is offered here. The list tallies closely with the practices for improving human welfare (above), since human well-being is entwined so inextricably with the welfare of the planet.

- **First,** we take "science" seriously, in school and throughout life. It is not just a "subject." It is the actual (and factual) explanation of the real world. It is, by definition, important and relevant to us, not to mention interesting. It is basic knowledge. Without it, we do not understand the world—or at least, our understanding is needlessly limited to our own observations and experience, which may be of great value, but which pale against the great body of wider knowledge which lies within easy reach. The more we know, the more effective we can be in making the natural world a better place.
- **Second,** we predispose ourselves to be active everyday players in maintaining and improving the environment around us. We recycle; we conserve water; we use

fuel-efficient vehicles; we minimize our reliance on herbicides and pesticides; we monitor and moderate our consumption of food and other goods, choosing products that are less likely to cause ecological harm, e.g. eating fish only from plentiful species, or selecting fabrics processed without environmentally-damaging chemicals. We tread gently. We restore damage if we can.

- Third, we carry our stewardship practices into our workplaces, our schools, and the other domains in which we live and work, and push to have them incorporated into the culture of these institutions and places. We take on some of the work this commitment requires.
- Fourth, we actually focus our vocation – or avocation – in a field which addresses the health of the environment and the species which inhabit it: environmental science and engineering; ecology; environmental law; wildlife or marine biology; oceanography; the geological and physical sciences; agronomy; forestry; natural resource management; and so many other fields. We *become* the experts and policy makers and practitioners.
- Fifth, we contribute financial support or sweat equity or lobbying efforts to organizations and projects which advance the well-being of the environment. And we support, speak out for, and vote for political candidates and propositions which help the cause.
- Sixth, we share our own access to beautiful or interesting or important natural places in order to introduce them to others, explain their special characteristics, and perhaps kindle a broader enthusiasm and support for their protection and enhancement.

The points above form a basic starter list—probably a familiar one. Yet it can be a useful discipline to set out a list such as this, in order to make goals more concrete, and the follow-through easier.

The Bonus of Betterment

Reviewing the chapters on "doing good" and "doing better"— on improving human and environmental well-being—we see the self-evident benefits in adopting good practice. But besides the obvious benefits, there may be "bonus points" for making beneficial contributions. In a competitive Real World, where we seek our own advantage—or our community's advantage—as well as the common good, consider the other incentives for good practice:

- **First**, the "improver" gains power, autonomy and control over the quality of his/her own life and environment.

- **Second**, the "improver" acquires local political power and prestige ("soft power" in the phrase of political scientist Joseph Nye) through success in advancing the well-being of the community, thereby increasing the appeal and attractiveness of his/her locality and practices to others inside and outside the community. (Nye, former Dean of the Kennedy School of Government at Harvard University, was Chairman of the National Intelligence Council and an Assistant Secretary of Defense in the Clinton administration. His concept of "soft power," referring to the attractive influence of a culture—distinguished from its military, political or economic power—has become an article of faith in discussions of international security and conflict resolution.)[124]

- **Third**, the "improver" may realize significant economic benefits from successful products or programs which improve human well-being and the environment.

- **Fourth**, there is a likelihood that efforts and success in improving the well-being of people and the natural world are contagious, and spur others to similar efforts (such as the "epidemic" of walks and bike-a-thons for human health or environmental causes).

- **Fifth**, on a global stage of political competition and adversity, the "improver" generates good will towards him/herself for positive achievements which have broader benefits – benefits which can extend beyond the local community to the region or possibly the world. He/she will be more welcome in the world outside.
- **Sixth**, the "improver" earns the intrinsic satisfaction of advancing the good of humanity and the world.

※ ※ ※

Chapter 14

Have Fun and Give Thanks

The last vital piece in the puzzle of Be-ism: appreciate and enjoy existence—the real universe—for its own sake. Reflect, have fun, give thanks. Take down-time, let go, create, socialize, entertain, amuse. Offer up work and worry (not so easy to do). Muse, take inventory, regroup, celebrate the goods. Learning and teaching, acting, doing good, doing better, are the work—how about the play? Not to be neglected.

The desire to enjoy is part of our nature. Humans have no monopoly on enjoyment: other species have their own versions. Any owner of a dog or cat—any observer of animals or birds—knows well their expressions of gratitude, contentment, joy, even ecstasy. A scene comes to mind: A robust young Pekingese dog at the edge of a long field, spying a large flock of Canada geese grazing at the far end, sounds one reverberating call, "WOOF!" Way down the field, ninety geese raucously take to flight, as one. The dog puffs out his chest, his brown eyes sparkle, and he prances back to his owner—tail flagged like an Arabian stallion—grinning from ear to ear. "Airs above the ground." Dog ecstasy.

We too. Responding to good feelings about ourselves and the world, we develop varied and complex ways of expressing our awareness and pleasure and gratitude. With tremendous imagination and zest we celebrate the people and the accomplishments and the situations—and the "existence" itself—which bring us joy. The act of celebration gives us cause, and a pause, for reflection and taking stock. It marks important milestones for us, cements our social compact with each other, affirms our common awareness of the beautiful and joy-bringing moments of life. And—not least important—the celebration becomes a cause in itself, enjoyable and amusing and edifying, fortifying greatly our sense of well-being and comradeship, and our pleasure in being alive.

The celebration idea, which includes our natural human response of *thankfulness,* raises a new challenge, for the Be-ist. We are so conditioned to the notion of a "giver" and a "givee." Aware of our extraordinary good fortune in having life, family, friends, community, and the great world and universe in which they exist, how do we express our contentment and satisfaction and elation at having all these things? *To whom* do we address our thanks and appreciation? Often in our experience there *is* a giver: a parent (who bore us, and gave us a home and love and guidance); a teacher (who gave us knowledge and tools of inquiry and inspiration); a civic leader or activist or philanthropist (who gave us clean water and National Parks and equal voting rights); a scientist (who gave us new cancer treatments and warnings of global warming and images of Saturn's moon).

But when it comes to being thankful for *existence itself*—for "the beauty of the earth," for our friends and loved ones and idols, for our own life and all that comes with it—whom do we thank? In this case, the "greatest things of all" are the result of an eons-old *process.* How can we express gratitude to a *process*? We can't and don't. We celebrate the process itself: "How Things Work," writ both large and small. The gleaming steel machines in Hershey, PA, that extrude the peanut butter into the little cups of chocolate; the green-and-gold cocooning and orange-and-black hatching of a Monarch butterfly on a milkweed leaf; and then, taken all together, the full-fledged workings of the cosmos itself. Reflecting on the cosmos, we are inexpressibly appreciative of its processes and its consequences, wowed by its extraordinary beauty, complexity, productivity. But there is no *object* of our gratitude. Perhaps the closest we can come is to thank our *good fortune* (our "lucky stars") for being included.

How our life "comes out" is a combination of *chance* (circumstance and processes over which we have no control) and our own *influence* (decisions, actions, behavior, attitudes taken by us). The "chance" part requires humility and a bit of detachment:

we cannot take the credit, nor assume the blame. If we have good fortune, we rejoice, with the joy of winning the lottery. If our luck is bad, we rail at fate. The "influence" part, on the other hand, calls for a genuine response of pride or shame, satisfaction or ambivalence: an honest reckoning of our influence on ourselves or others, for better or worse. Be-ism requires the grace to accept our fortune, and the motivation to make the most of it: turning advantages to good use, from lemons making lemonade.

To recognize the good in life, and to celebrate it (never to take it for granted), is to acknowledge the great worth—the good fortune—of our existence. In this sense, celebrations also are an expression of our humility, and our underlying realization that no good can be taken for granted. Because of the great role which chance plays in every aspect of existence, we never *know* what the future will bring. When, through the combination of chance and our own actions and the actions of others, the future brings "good," we understand that we have cause for celebration. We feel joy, and the need to express it, especially because we have *not* taken anything for granted. To share this sense of appreciation with our fellow humans is to reinforce the deep bond which ties us to each other and to existence itself.

Because life is uncertain, we also know that sometimes the combination of chance (in this case, bad fortune), and the action or inaction of ourselves and others, will cause harm or suffering, pain or loss, damage or disaster, to ourselves and to the real world. We recognize the bad events by mourning, grieving, expressing our sympathy and apology and shame and regret in many different ways. We are painfully aware of our insufficiency. But we always are striving to learn more – to figure out how to avoid doing more harm, and how to mitigate or reverse damage that has already been done by us, or others, or "chance": natural disasters such as earthquakes or volcanic eruptions or droughts or plagues, which still are beyond our control. The enormous (and petty) problems and challenges of existence in a far-from-perfect world remind us constantly that we must have humility and forbearance. On some missions (eliminating human poverty, stopping the scourge of destructive illegal drugs—the Chicago Cubs winning the World Series) we try and fail, try and fail, try and fail again. On the other hand, our many successes (some of them brilliant), throughout a long human history of trying to overcome danger and suffering and weakness and misery, have taught us that our struggles can bear fruit. Because each success—and the goods we enjoy because of it—is a consequence of so much human effort, and also has won in the dicey lottery of chance, it is doubly worthy of celebration. We acknowledge the human effort and the luck. We are overjoyed at the good, grateful to those who made it happen, and "thank our lucky stars" at the crucial role played by chance. The successes give us the motivation and optimism to keep trying for more. A celebration of success marks the achievement, fixes it in our memory, re-inspires us to move forward.

Life is rich with opportunity for fun and appreciation. Enjoying it is an art more than a "practice." But in the context of "the manual," we can survey the possibilities, to remind ourselves of their diversity and their huge capacity to give us pleasure of so many kinds.

Time Out

We crave a break, off and on, from the effort and stress and time pressure of everyday life—time to slow down, observe, take stock, exist. Smell the lilacs. Watch the tide turn. How do we step out of the mania, the frenzy, the hectic pace of modern life? How do we achieve a measure of *distance* and *detachment*, to gain perspective and restore balance?

As a culture we accommodate leisure by building in regulated work hours, weekends, holidays, personal days, vacations, leaves-of-absence, sabbaticals. And eventually, retirement. But as a culture we also tend to feel chronically deprived of adequate down time. So perhaps what we have built in is not enough, and perhaps we could optimize, for leisure, the leisure time we are allotted.

With elective time at our disposal, how do we use it? Doing what we like to do, if possible—enjoying our avocations—either alone or in company. In summer we converge with family and friends on the beach or in the mountains; swim and hike; read a novel; go to the movies. At other seasons or leisure moments we travel or ski or fish; go to a ballgame or a concert or a pub; surf the internet; construct the SuperInterGalactic StarshipObliterator with Legos. But what about "thinking" leisure—the chance to consider our current life. Is our life satisfying? If not, what are some options? How are we doing at appreciating what we *do* have (even if it is not glamorous or dramatic or out of the ordinary)? To be able to relish the common beauty at our own front door is a step in the right direction. To see significance—or even magnificence—in it, is a greater leap of intellect and insight.

One challenge to an active mind is how to turn it off (and provide a respite, for not only ourselves, but our companions). Another challenge is to learn to exist in "real time," tuning out the past and the future, experiencing fully the moment. But a third challenge—perhaps the greatest – is to develop a satisfactory mode of reflection; of consolidating and synthesizing the "bigger picture" of our life and our world view; of achieving perspective, making sense of our own existence in the context of all existence. For in Be-ism, the problem is not "the abyss." It is the opposite: overwhelming complexity and teeming existence everywhere. Astrophysicists and cosmologist are surmising that even the void—the "nothingness" of deep space – actually vibrates with existence, pulsing with "strings" of energy. How do we ramp down?
Take a timeout from – and make sense of – this overload of *being*? How do we find order in the complexity, and reduce it to manageable terms in our mind?

Along with the complexity come confusing changes to our traditional perception of wholes and their parts. Disciplines and regions which used to be disparate now interconnect and overlap with a fluidity which makes it hard to follow the flow of knowledge and events. New categories form and old ones are no longer meaningful. Discussing major developments in academia since the 1980s, Harvard history professor Alison Frank (specializing in modern Europe) cites a "truly major change" in the way scholars regard the idea of "the nation." "Scholars are taking a transnational approach to their subjects.... more and more people feel a need to demonstrate that they're not constricted by national borders."[125] Convergence is everywhere.

And how do we avoid the whirlpool of *conventional* thought? We resolve to think originally, but before we know it, we are drawn back in, flailing among the old circular arguments that have trapped us before. We succumb to the pull of the retrospective—rehashing old views and ideas—and never get to the prospective. The whirlpool—more like a Jacuzzi—is warm and stimulating but we lose ourselves in the steam and bubbles. How do we manage to move back, step out the door, breathe the air? Look forward, clear our mind, "think fresh"?

Without invoking mystical help (religion, prayer) as we perhaps were taught, and no longer "believing," how do we achieve calm, clarity and forbearance against the complexity and relentless motion of life? Here we can try various techniques and disciplines—self control of our intellect and emotion, and even our heartbeat and breathing. People have been doing this (and needing to do it, and looking for better ways) for thousands of years. We can learn *techniques* of control from some religious practices (Buddhism and Quakerism come to mind), without subscribing to the mystical beliefs. Meditation, contemplation, narrowing of attention to a single neutral or positive object, slow deep breathing, sanctuary from noise and confusion and demands, physical exercise, and adjustments to our diet can help us attain calm. New research and discoveries in the art and science of self-healing reveal that we can take our mental health and tranquility into our own hands in ways we have not fully appreciated in modern times. Some of the knowledge is ancient, but only recently rediscovered in "advanced" societies.

The French psychiatrist David Servan-Schreiber, an experienced and respected practitioner of mainstream medicine and psychiatry, has led a growing number of physicians in his field to take seriously the study of ancient healing techniques, finding they are validated by new discoveries about the interaction of the human sympathetic and parasympathetic nervous systems, heart and brain. Meditation and other mind-control strategies and diet adjustments can help restore healthy balance to a heart-brain-nervous system that is out of whack and causing depression or stress.[126]

In 2006 Bruno Cantigiani, a harried Milanese businessman, engaged (and later married!) Ella, a "life coach," to help him slow down and find happiness. Together they have founded "L'Arte del Vivere con Lentezza" (The Art of Living Slowly). In 2007 they instituted a new holiday, the Global Day of Slow Living—celebrated mostly in Italy the first year. Visiting Manhattan in the winter of 2008, Contigiani wrote about The Reservoir in Central Park, "Take the time to walk around the … lake, do not run, simply walk. However, do it counterclockwise. You will realize that Central Park is a sort of old alarm clock, with an external ring, wound up by the people running around the lake." One of his slow-down tips: "Write your text messages on your cell phone with no symbols or abbreviations and get in the habit of starting with 'Dear…..'." [127]

We admire traditional cultures—usually rural, village, family-based or tribal societies—for the relative peacefulness, calmness, "easy" sense of life which they seem to have mastered, and we wonder how they do it. They live by subtle, unfamiliar, elusive (to us) practices, which modern society seems to have lost in the rush of material progress. But at last, by rediscovering and paying attention to their ways, we are uncovering some of the secrets of their success. If we observe yet more carefully, surely we can learn more from them.

We know we can achieve some calmness and peace—give the active brain a rest—through all five senses. A few simple examples:

- **Hearing:** Turn down the noise (*!*). Enjoy, at a *low* volume, the sound of music, or bird chatter, or wind in the trees, or rainfall. Resist listening to others' conversations, and enjoy for a change just the *sound* of voices conversing. Get out the rake, not the peace-shattering air-blasting (energy guzzling) leaf blower. Try—sometimes, somehow—for some moments of *complete* silence.

- **Sight:** Take in, slowly, some calm scene or object or image: a landscape, a tranquil figure, a shell, a harmonious or pleasing pattern or design. Or occasionally cancel the "incoming" altogether—eyes closed, lights off.
- **Smell:** Breathe in slowly the outside air (the better for pine woods, a meadow, the ocean, the desert, the mountains). *Do* smell the lilacs and honeysuckle—and cinnamon buns and fresh coffee, and wood smoke, and sweet incense.
- **Taste:** Try some "feel good" food and drink: a steaming bowl of cereal or soup; a mug of hot tea or chocolate (chocolate in any form?); a cool lemonade or a fresh gelato. Occasional fasting also is good: abstaining, paring down the intake.
- **Touch:** Seek out sun and sand, warm water, soft grass. Submit to it (!). Sign up for a massage. Get close with a friend or a brother or a lover (or a lap cat, or a gently snoring dog). Or—as with the other senses— take a full break from "touch."

The calming, even healing, role of the senses comes from their relaxed engagement with sight or smell or sound or food or fellow creature; and also, from disengagement. They can be turned on to a soothing stimulus, or turned off for a rest. Meanwhile, our brain takes the opportunity to reboot. Knowing a few calming tricks, and practicing the art of self-calming and detachment, we can live more *deliberately* (as Thoreau determined to do at Walden Pond). At the same time, we can choose not to be so hard on ourselves and others, to think and live more "easily." To lighten up. We can learn self-mastery, and teach it and foster it *as a matter of course* in our children and grandchildren and students.

Another discipline endangered by the frenzy and self-absorption of modern life is the practice of intellectual detachment, of thinking impersonally. Do we become inclined, in our self-centric way, to assume that the world depends on *us*—on *our* personal views and experience? In Stephen Crane's well-known lines,

> A man said to the Universe,
> "Sir I exist."
> "However," replied the universe,
> "The fact has not created in me
> A sense of obligation."

Emerson observed in his journal, "All thoughts of a turtle are turtle."

Would our stress level drop if we could damp down our presumption, and comprehend that the rest of existence (including most of humankind) is generally *neutral* with respect to our own life? That the world generally is indifferent to our existence, does not care one way or the other, except when we pose a clear benefit or imminent threat? We use the resources of the planet to sustain or improve the quality of our own life. The turtle—and our neighbors in the next town, and in Outer Mongolia—are doing the same (likewise, the Ebola virus). Perhaps it would relieve us of some of the "weight" of existence if we could refrain from exaggerating our indispensability, the assumption that all other life forms, and the rest of our fellow humans, *depend* on us all day every day. (At the same time, of course—acknowledging *some* responsibility—we will continue our efforts to protect and preserve ourselves, our species and our habitat, the earth.)

In sorting out thoughts and beliefs, a community of thoughtful family, friends and colleagues is helpful and sometimes vital to us. But in the end it is solitary work. It is a personal mission, and each of us must go alone. We need society but we also need solitude, to discover what we "really think." We must learn, on our own, how to find calm and tranquility, how to breathe the air, how to know our place, how to savor existence and live it the best way we can. And if we are fortunate, we will succeed not only in "knowing ourselves," but in finding good sympathetic like-minded company with whom to share life. (Even if we're abandoned on a desert isle like Tom Hanks in the film "Cast Away," and all we have for companionship is "Wilson," the volleyball.)

Rule 6: Laugh at Yourself.
"I am my own comedy and tragedy."
-- Emerson, Journal, March 1833

There is always the enticing pastime of *disparaging* existence—our own corner of it or the whole thing: the challenges, the struggles, the flops and failures; the pathos (as in "pathetic") of our shames and embarrassments; the appalling stupidity of us and everyone else; our ineptness and cluelessness; our narcissism and grandiosity and greed; our gullibility and deceitfulness; our flakiness and obsessiveness; our insecurity and cowardice; our earnestness and boastfulness; our gender sensibilities; our overall neediness. With luck, we can see the ridiculousness of it all—relish (sometimes) the *blight* of existence. The Life you Love to Hate. We like company in our misery. In comradely angst, we wince at the ironies and absurdities and hypocrisy and bad breaks of life. It's the human "comedy." It's the price of being self-aware, and knowing our neighbors as well as ourselves.

Humor makes us laugh, but it also reveals an understanding of life, of "getting it." The good cartoonist and the stand-up comic wield a special talent for getting to the quick of the matter, for exposing the foibles of humanity and the weirdness of life, for bursting the balloon. Motivated by a compulsion to reveal the *truth* behind the *appearance*, the satirists can serve as honest brokers for society. Gary Trudeau makes us wince and groan as we follow "ourselves" (and our politicians) in the daily "Doonesbury" strip. Maureen Dowd zings all and sundry from her *New York Times* column: she doesn't really care who is in her sights—just likes to "tweak power." Likewise the late great Texan Molly Ivins, speaking truth to power with her killer one-liners.[128] The best and wittiest have an instinct not only for homing in on phoniness, pretension, contradiction, and all kinds of bad or ridiculous behavior, but — even more admirable—for being able to offer it to us like a piece of cake.

The brand of humor we respond to says a lot about our own history and our waxing and waning maturity as a culture: in recent times, the crass crudity and relentless in-your-face putdowns from comedy-club TV and films like "Borat"; earlier, Woody Allen (still holding on), with his hip urban fatalism and little-guy neurosis; the incomparable Erma Bombeck, on suburban-mom angst; Yogi Berra and Casey Stengel on Baseball-and-Life; Bob Hope, from the "Greatest Generation," with the sideways grin and the sly one-liner, getting a roaring reception from GI's in a distant war zone; Mark Twain and Will Rogers in a still earlier age, with their deadpan take-offs on pretentious townfolk in the country—and all the way back to Aristophanes. As a sampler of modern humor, a few thoughts on "death:"

> For her tombstone: "I told you I was sick." (Erma Bombeck)
> "I'm not afraid of death. I just don't want to be there when it happens." (Woody Allen)
> "When I die, I want to go peacefully in my sleep, like my grandfather...not screaming and yelling, like the passengers in his car." (Unknown)
> "It is often said that before you die your life passes before your eyes. It is in fact true. It's called living." (Terry Pratchett)
> "# ! # !
> # the # -ing ** !" (Late Night comic, generic).
> (It does have a certain cadence to it....)

Contemporary "adult" humor fixates on sex and scatology, and on the (sometimes vicious) putdown of just about anything, often including the comedian's audience. This is not a new phenomenon—crude humor, too, goes back a few thousand years. Late-night slots in comedy are reserved for "mature" audiences. Interesting, what passes for mature humor: the Cartoon Network's popular late-night show "Aqua Teen Hunger Force" stars a talking box of French fries, with cameo appearances by little video game characters who grimace and make obscene gestures. Small lightboard mockups of the rudely gesturing little figures brought the city of Boston, MA, to a standstill on a January evening in 2007, when the boards were discovered attached to bridges and buildings, and were thought to be a bomb hoax. In the predictable deluge of media coverage of the "scare," there was little or no comment on the image itself, so inured are we to the rude gesture and its ability to get a laugh.

Religion itself is always a popular butt of ridicule, by its practitioners as well as the bystanders. But in recent times, with religious extremism taking a drastic toll on world harmony, and deep internal scandals rocking some religions, the humor has become darker and more hard-hitting. Serious and widespread jibes at the "serious" institutions of the churches may or may not signal lasting damage to the regard in which they are held by contemporary society.

We don't know what's coming down next. Could a shift in our attitude to life and existence—our values and priorities—generate a new and more "evolved" humor, a touch more subtle and insightful, a bit more empathetic and forgiving? Irony in place of sarcasm? Wit instead of crudity? Wryness rather than contempt? A few genuine laughs—less of the pained wince—at those celebrity roasts? For *comedy* does require at least an iota of empathy or sympathy; otherwise, it is not humor at all, but something else—rage or resentment or vindictiveness—masquerading as humor. Do we still laugh along? Do we know the difference?

On the plus side, a *New Yorker* cartoon still can make us chuckle; there's "Doonesbury" and a number of the other strips; some of the blogs are downright witty; there are the unquenchable wiseguys among our family and friends and office-mates; Click and Clack, the Tappet Brothers, make cars (and people who own cars) funny; and there are always the "Lucy" and Redd Foxx re-runs. Just keep them coming....

Play

What's play? "Not work"? Does it have to be one or the other: *work* is "virtuous but no fun," and *play,* the opposite? The Puritan distinction—that if it's *enjoyable* it can't be *work*—creates an artificial dichotomy. The Be-ist stance—that any action which makes a net contribution to well-being is *good,* and any which causes a net loss is *bad*—lets us rethink the concept of "work versus play," and banish the old guilt. Reflection and enjoyment and celebration, when they give genuine enjoyment, are vital to a full life. They are as worthy as knowledge, work, and "good works."

New neuroscience tells us more about the nature and role of play. The scientist Jaak Panksepp of Bowling Green State University has found neural circuitry that primes us for play and also for joy:

> "Identical circuitry for playfulness can be found in all mammals, including the ubiquitous laboratory mouse. This tract hides in the most ancient neural zones, down in the brain stem ... that governs reflexes and our most primordial responses."

Play "seems to have a vital role in a child's neural growth," and it can only happen where the child feels safe and protected. (Panksepp even suggests that if young children were allowed to "vent" regularly through rough-and tumble play, there would be less ADHD—that children are being deprived of necessary play, and therefore are unable to focus adequately on their work.)[129] As the brain matures, the prefrontal area becomes fully wired, and we are better able to "get serious;" but still we continue to channel our energy into enjoyable pastimes, and never lose altogether the sense of play.

Sometimes the concept of "fun" and "play" goes bad. We overstep the line between moderation and excess—in drink, drugs, music, video games, food, sex, or some other pleasure. In *Female Chauvinist Pigs* (unfortunate book title), the *New York Magazine* writer Ariel Levy describes the spring break "raunch" culture (epitomized by the late night TV show *Girls Going Wild*), where vacationing co-eds, disinhibited by drink and drugs, succumb to party-crowd encouragement and strip in public in front of the TV cameras. The ritual is a rite of passage gone awry, manipulated by the cynical operatives of commercial interests who are promoting an exhibitionist culture. The young female participants, their judgment impaired by alcohol and peer pressure, are persuaded to trade their integrity for a moment of celebrity. They are hyped into a sense of "nothing to lose"—an illusion of "ultimate freedom"—when in fact what they lose is great: their self-respect and their integrity, their sense of intactness and dignity. The next day, they can't get it back. "For women, and only women, hotness requires projecting a kind of eagerness, offering a promise that any attention you receive for your physicality is welcome."[130]

Keeping a reasonable grip on the appetite for pleasure and play has been a challenge since the beginning of time, and probably always will be. But it may become easier to manage, as we understand more about the influences working on us and on each other, from both the inside and the outside, for and against our own well-being.

Arts and Entertainment

For the artist and the observer (listener or watcher or reader), the great human universe of the interpretive and expressive and creative arts is a marvel in its own right—a grandly rich, diverse and provocative creation by us, about us, and about existence as we have experienced it for the past several thousand years. It is a magnificent human-created body of original work. Our art is testament to the extraordinary awareness and sensitivity of our species with regard to ourselves and the planet and the cosmos we inhabit. It is proof of our power—and our insatiable impulse—to express this awareness and sensitivity and communicate it to our fellows, using all our senses and our physical, intellectual and emotional abilities, enabled and stimulated by our civilization's remarkable accumulation of achievements in knowledge and technology.

In the 1940s the British dancer Frederic Franklin, now-legendary star of the Ballet Russe de Monte Carlo, imported to the USA a new performance sensation: modern dance. Sixty years later, in 2007, Franklin visited Jacob's Pillow, the American Ballet Theater's summer workshop in the Berkshires in upstate New York. Still brimming with vigor and pizzaz at ninety-three, he regaled the rapt young dancers with tales of his long career. And he confided that his great joy and satisfaction in the world has come from a lifetime of doing, and improving on, and relishing, what he loves and does best: dance. With contagious ardor, the venerable Franklin pressed his point—and surely a new generation of dancers carried the message home.

Beauty and the Be-ist.

Through the art of language—poetry, novels, narratives, drama – we use words to express the inestimable beauty of the world; and also with paint and pen and sculpture, built forms and dance and music, theatre and opera. The extreme beauty of the words (the painting, the dance, the music, the architecture) tends to strike us as almost tragic: in our inability to absorb it; in its transience; in its power of metaphor for actual existence; in its contrast to the darker elements with which it coexists. It transports us out of ourselves. Emerson (as poet) discovers in the waters of the Concord River not one, but "Two Rivers:"

"So forth and brighter flows my stream –
Who drinks it shall not thirst again.
No darkness stains its equal gleam,
And ages drop in it like rain."

We look for, recognize, draw deep pleasure from beauty in its many forms—in the arts but also, throughout our lives, in our daily experience. It perhaps is as close as we get, through our senses and our emotions and our intellect, to the "optimums" of existence. We know it when we see it (hear it, smell it, taste it—feel it). Many kinds of beauty catch our attention, chaos and wildness and extravagance among them: Niagara Falls booming onto the rocks below, a black squall at sea, the floats at Mardi Gras. At the other end of the spectrum, we respond almost psychically to the spare elegance of symmetry and order—either static order or an orderly process. It seems to represent for us a pure principle of physical existence (as with the laws of geometry or physics); it triggers a sensation of joy and inspiration and reassurance. It satisfies our spirit when we understand it, catch on, solve the puzzle— Einstein discovering that $E=MC^2$, or we on the commuter bus solving the daily Sudoku. Edna St. Vincent Millay, in an untitled sonnet about the mathematician Euclid, describes such beauty:

> Euclid alone has looked on Beauty bare.
> Let all who prate of Beauty hold their peace,
> And lay them prone upon the earth and cease
> To ponder on themselves, the while they stare
> At nothing, intricately drawn nowhere
> In shapes of shifting lineage; let geese
> Gabble and hiss, but heroes seek release
> From dusty bondage into luminous air.
> O blinding hour, O holy, terrible day,
> When first the shaft into his vision shone
> Of light anatomized! Euclid alone
> Has looked on Beauty bare. Fortunate they
> Who, though once only and then but far away,
> Have heard her massive sandal set on stone.[131]

Paradoxically, we also discover that when pursued *as an end in itself,* when excessively *self* conscious, beauty loses its full luster and its ability to stir, and at the same time generates in us some anxiety and a sense of voyeurism (as in watching the self-conscious and highly-orchestrated glitz of the beauty pageant, or the ritual spectacle of the "red carpet" as the glitterati go on parade).

Through the arts we express—or discern— not only beauty but a full range of speculations, imaginings, fantasies, observations, questions, convictions, passions, sympathies, confusions, rages, fears, hopes and aspirations. Not content with mere language, or body language, to communicate observations and views and aesthetics, we turn to theatre, film, TV, music, painting, drawing, architecture, sculpture, poetry, fiction, dance, and performance art. We express our personal selves–our style, our "attitude," our social identity–in the art of our dress and possessions; the design of our clothes; the cut and color of our hair; our choice of cosmetics and fragrances; our adornment with accessories and bling. Our aesthetic sense reveals itself in the décor of our home or dorm room or cubicle; in our preference for particular flowers or trees or landscaping; in the music we play; in our ceremonial preparation and presentation of food and drink.

The arts are a record of our social and cultural, religious and political history, and our human response to this history, and our lessons learned from it. The lyrics and sound of contemporary popular music—folk, country, jazz, R&B, rock and roll, rap, hip hop—say a lot about modern times, and today's culture and concerns. The younger generation, who seek and crave authenticity, who have a big appetite for reality (plus the normal preoccupation with love and heartbreak), express themselves—and entertain themselves—through a near-obsession with music. The songs they listen to—playing all day long on the iPods and on the radio—are songs about real life and longing, secular themes (for the most part) of love and loss, rebellion and craziness, hardship and "getting along." Nothing really new, but something very "real."

Then there is the dance. Modern dance—among the most "live and tuned" of all the arts—delivers a powerful up-to-date commentary on contemporary society. Back in the 1940s, Fred Franklin arrived in Manhattan with the dazzling then-new choreography of the Ballet Russe. Six decades later, in December 2006—also in Manhattan—the Bill T. Jones/Arnie Zane Dance Company unleashed on a contemporary audience a new dance, "Chapel/Chapter," at the Gatehouse, a former water pumping station for New York City (now an adjunct performance space for Harlem Stage).

"Mr. Jones has transformed [the space], draping [it] in heavy red curtains. With a white floor pattern that looks like a cross between a flat cathedral window and a shuffleboard court, and the audience seated on all four sides of the rectangular performing area, the "chapel" part of the title is clear. 'Chapter' is less clear, but the visceral impact of the piece is inescapable.

The dance lasts 70 minutes and has at its core three stories: the mass murder of a family of four, a father's killing of his 'troubled' daughter, and the tale of two 11-year-old boys who sneak away from their camp tent to watch the sunrise....

These stories are picked up and examined like stones, or stone shards. ...They appear as print on the floor. They are sun. And they are danced, with a brilliant blend of abstraction and realistic evocation....

Overlying the stories is our court and prison system, yet it is never portrayed as racist (the cast is particularly diverse) or as an instrument of capitalist oppression....

Rarely has [Mr. Jones] been better able to sublimate his wide-ranging political, social and moral concerns into art. Rarely has the strength of that art made his vision express itself more purely."[132]

And as in dance, the medium of film projects a broad reflection—with wide screen and surround sound—of the issues and attitudes of contemporary society. Far more than in dance, the level and volume of violence in films has escalated in recent times.

The critics mount a gallant effort to parse the often savage dramas which equate with "entertainment" in Hollywood (and increasingly, Bollywood) today: to ferret out the art and the message in the sometimes-horrific stories, and to explain—sometimes defend—their huge appeal at the box office. On the same day as the review of "Chapel/Chapter," the *New York Times* carried an analysis by the critic David Carr, "Stalking Oscar, with Carnage and Mayhem Galore."

> "…this year an unusual amount of mayhem is showing up in the movies… Academy members in the thick of screening for the Oscars could be forgiven for wishing they had donned surgical scrubs for what has become a very bloody year.…
>
> …many [films] include overtly violent themes that are executed with jaw-dropping visual candor.

Carr goes on to describe the year's war and crime movies ("The Departed," "Flags of Our Fathers"); and message movies ("Blood Diamond," showing child amputees; "The Last King of Scotland" with human flesh "regarded as a cut of beef;" "Apocalypto" with "human hearts held aloft… and enough impalement to bring to mind human shish kebab.") He quotes Robert Rosen, dean of the School of theater, Film and Television at UCLA:

> "There is increasingly a choreography of violence, a way of aestheticizing it, that makes it more acceptable and worthy of recognition. In a way graphic violence in films has become a displaced expression of the violence that is always there in the real world, just offstage."

Then film historian David Thomsen weighs in:

> "There are extraordinary cruelties out there in the real world…and I think that's why torture has come into our entertainments in a serious way. There is a truthfulness to it that audiences seem to be responding to."

Maybe so. But "extraordinary cruelties" have been out there in the real world throughout human history. Do we have a newly awakened need to know—and perhaps confront—the "awful truths" about life? Or are we using mayhem gratuitously as "entertainment" in a life which otherwise is rather tame— which does *not* feature genocide just around our own particular corner. And are we perhaps preparing ourselves in case the distant dangers, hyped daily on CNN and Fox News, should close in on us too. In any case, it seems that we humans are capable of many varieties of "enjoyment," as delivered to us by an extraordinary diversity of arts.

The arts enrich our experience of life directly and vicariously. Through them we stay alive to the pulse of our culture and other cultures. Through our own art, if it is strong and original and authentic, we may influence the pulse itself, and change (for the better, one would hope) the way our community looks at—and sees—itself and the cosmos.

Avocations: "For their own sake"

We like to do what we like to do. Our avocations counterbalance our work life. Left to our own devices and given the resources and time, we follow them. If well suited to us – our innate ability and our natural inclination—they enhance our satisfaction and sense of self. They also convey something about us to others, usually something that we would be pleased to have others know. (If not, that raises a question in itself.) As in the arts, we pursue avocations as a participant, an observer, or both. Sometimes, our pleasure as an *observer* of work within our avocation—whether portrait painting or farm machinery or mushroom culture—can be comparable to (or exceed) the satisfaction of having done the work ourselves. We experience a palpable "lift" from good work generated by our fellows. Success, prowess, innovation, beauty and style are strong motivators. They confirm our hope that ingenuity and style and skill and perseverance are alive and well in the culture.

Dominant among contemporary avocations are sports, both playing (non-professionally) and following them: pickup basketball in the parking lot; season tickets to the Knicks or the Chargers; NASCAR; bowling; coaching soccer; hiking and kayaking; skateboarding and rollerblading. The huge choice available to us in sports and recreational activities, whether as player or spectator, is a powerful statement of the value that we, even as a modern society, still attach to physical action. Along with the thrill of victory and the agony of defeat—our own or that of the home team—sports bring opportunity for intense friendships and camaraderie, the honing and enjoyment of social as well as physical skills. And (except for the six-packs and the fries in the stadium seats) they have the obvious benefit of enhancing our health and fitness.

Also included by definition as avocations are all our hobbies: chess, antiquing, shopping, quilt-making, crossword puzzles, blogging, nature study, stamp collecting, gardening, bird-watching. Except when practiced as a profession, the arts fall into this category, too: painting and drawing; photography and playing the guitar; ballroom dancing and writing poetry and shooting video. All are ways to express ourselves, deploy our talent, indulge our desires.

And then, the "avocation" (if you can call it that) of eating and drinking: foodie culture, micro-breweries, designer coffee. It's a rich pleasure: the food and drink, the ambience—the staff, the décor, the music, the buzz—the camaraderie. We have our neighborhood Joe, of the Bar & Grill. And then, catering to our expanding tastes, the cafes and bistros, the pubs and restaurants, featuring menu and cuisine, décor and music, chef and servers from China, Thailand, Brazil, Morocco, France, Italy, Ireland, India, Mexico—many within a twenty-minute radius of home. Local and global pleasure in wining and dining.

Another favorite avocation: travel. (Where to begin...) Why? To satisfy our strong desire to move, to get out of town, to indulge an insatiable curiosity about the world: its landscapes and seascapes and climates, people and cuisine, flora and fauna; its cities and villages, arts and sports, languages and cultures. We want to see for ourselves where and how other people live. We want to meet them. (Carol Elk, a visit coordinator at the Japanese Travel Bureau in New York City, makes arrangements for Japanese visitors to Manhattan—Yankees tickets, MOMA exhibits, Broadway shows. But also, a request that she gets frequently: "to have dinner at home with a regular American family.")[133] We want "them" to see "us" as well. We want to find the differences and the similarities, and we may be disposed to relish both. On our return, we want to share with others the high points and discoveries (and of course, the horrors and disasters). As the world becomes more physically interconnected—the means of travel and communication fast, diverse, efficient and affordable—pleasure travel has exploded into a global phenomenon and a lucrative global industry. As with sports and recreation and dining, the enormous choice in travel opportunities reveals how very much we enjoy seeing the world (and how much the world welcomes our visits, or at least our dollars and euros and yen). We want the unknown to become known to us directly. Travel brings great rewards, social and intellectual, aesthetic and physical. The world beckons and we go.

In thinking about avocations (as above), we know the distinction between avocation and vocation tends to blur. What if we make a livelihood doing something that we like, or even feel passionate about or compelled to do (as for a professional musicians, a software engineer, a heart surgeon)? On the other hand, even avocations are not unmixed pleasure: they often include hardship, extremes of effort, injuries, or disappointments (a failed attempt on Mt. Everest; losing the game on errors; ruining the almost-finished watercolor; camping in the cold pouring rain).

Society

If the heart of human society is its entwined social connections, a basic measure of the "success" of the society is the vitality, richness, and satisfactoriness of its social culture to its people. Sociologists, psychologists and psychiatrists; anthropologists, behavioral scientists and social historians document and analyze and explain to us the latest knowledge and speculation about how our societies function. The social scientists, in league with the neuroscientists, continually reveal new discoveries about the power and the idiosyncrasies of human affiliation.

Because it is a subject of enormous interest to us—because our individual identity and well-being and our very survival depend on how we live together—society surely will continue to pursue unabated the eons-old quest to understand the dynamics of human relationships. The literature on the subject is very large. But here, in a short summary, is a simple overview of social culture, and the most common social relations which enrich our enjoyment and celebration of life and the world.

First, we acknowledge the essential role of human affection itself in giving us a sense of well-being in the world. We need each other's affection and care. Deprived of it, we wither. We are a social species, like it or not, and we rely on each other for happiness. We take pleasure and stimulation, satisfaction and security, from all kinds and degrees of social ties. If fortune is good to us, we enjoy the extreme experience of affection, love. We prize it as the highest bond, encompassing social affection but everything else as well—the *omniphilia* mentioned earlier. It expresses the full measure of our affinity for the universe itself. Our affection, sparked by the special object of desire—another human being, a painting, a mountain range, a yacht, a horse, a symphony—casts a glow on the whole cosmos. The philosopher Emerson says it the other way around: "Love draws might from terrine force and potencies of sky."[134]

Most of us want a mate, a partner. Most of us want a marriage: a lifelong partnership, the formation of a family of our own. Society can't get enough of "the mating game"—the underlying or explicit subject of most of our fiction, theater, music, and dance (not to mention print advertising, TV commercials and tabloid gossip). Courting and mating, the sex-driven relationships, obviously are crucial to the propagation of humankind. And understandably, they dominate (or at least figure large in) our own social relations from the start to the conclusion of our search for a mate. Once we succeed (if we find a "good" one), we generally leave the game to those who still are looking. (We do enjoy being spectators to their shenanigans—or sometime accomplices or a shoulder to cry on—but not to the exclusion of other interests.) If we lose our own mate, we probably try again, and once again the search may dominate our social life. But the social interactions of courting and mating, although high in intensity and significance at the time, figure ultimately as a small fraction of the whole social experience of most of us. Even when the tie to our partner is paramount, we have other compelling social needs as well—for kinship, friendship, non-romantic love, camaraderie, collegiality, fellowship and respect.

A reverse measure of the power of our affection—and our anticipation of future affection—is the depth of our sadness when we lose someone dear to us, and thereby lose also the prospects they hold for us. The columnist David Brooks quotes the cognitive scientist Douglas Hofstadter, who lost his wife Carol to a brain tumor:

> "[A]t the core of both our souls lay our identical hopes and dreams for our children.....those hopes were not separate or distinct hopes but were just one hope, one clear thing that defined us both, that welded us into a unit, the kind of unit I had but dimly imagined before being married and having children."

Hofstadter's hard-won revelation was that a *self* is "a point of view, a way of seeing the world. It emerges from the conglomeration of all the flares, loops and perceptions that have been shared and developed with others.... a social, dynamic, overlapping theory of self." Brooks concludes,

> "It's not exactly new to say that no man is an island. But Hofstadter is one of hundreds of scientists and scholars showing how interconnectedness actually works. What's being described is a vast web of information—some contained in genes, some in brain structure, some in the flow of dinner conversation—that joins us to our ancestors and reminds the living of the presence of the dead." [135]

The pain is profound whether we suffer a loss through death; illness (especially mental disorders such as dementia or bipolar syndrome or schizophrenia); geographical separation; or the loss of reciprocity or "exclusivity" of affection (the defection of a loved one through infidelity, or by the reversal or diminishment of their affection for us). Although we grieve most the loss of a mate or family member or friend or colleague, we mourn also those whom we know only indirectly, or via a news story or an obituary or the grapevine. Our empathy is so strong that the death or hard fortune of a stranger can strike us as a tangible personal loss. Likewise the death or suffering of a pet or an animal we don't even "know." We even mourn the demise of a house plant or a shrub or a tree—let alone a forest or a natural landscape.

How do we use to best effect the sometimes-hard-won understanding (of the strength of our human bonds)? Perhaps by learning that the bonds cannot be taken for granted: that we had better appreciate and nurture them as we go; that we are wise to maintain a modicum of detachment from those we like and love—in their interest and our own – so as not to become too needy in, and of, the relationship; that we enjoy our *reliance* on friends and colleagues and loved ones without letting reliance turn into excessive *dependence*; that we accept that all our bonds are "of this world."

Socializing helps us accumulate "social capital" and "moral capital," in terms used by Robert Putnam in *Bowling Alone,* and Michael Shermer (publisher of *Skeptic* and author of *Why Darwin Matters). Social capital* is "social networks and the norms of reciprocity and trustworthiness that arise from them." *Moral capital* is "the connections within an individual between morality and behavior."[136] Taking part in civic life builds social capital. Our success in restraining aggression and inappropriate sexual behavior builds moral capital.[137] Both are vital to the health of our societies. And we have cause for optimism, because the coming generation, the Millennials—unlike their predecessors the Boomers—seem already to be distinguishing themselves as a group by their strong sense of affiliation and community, and their disinclination to "bowl alone."[138]

In social celebrations, we mark personal milestones: baby showers, birthdays, coming-of-age events, graduations, weddings, promotions, retirements, and memorial services. They are family centered, or work centered, or include friends and acquaintances and the community. The celebrations rekindle and foster the connections among us. They remind us of each other's attractive qualities and promising potential. They confirm that we value each other. Through them we acknowledge each other's progress through life, achievements in education and at work, and role in supporting the family and the community. Enjoyed in the right spirit, they are occasions for humor, affection, congratulation, inspiration, reminiscence, reconciliation, and recommitment − not to mention nice presents, gala food, good music, and maybe dancing or other amusing diversions. They affirm and celebrate our affinity for each other and for life.

Once in a while a participant—inadvertently or not—will taint a celebration with tactless behavior or remarks. The occasion can thus be spoiled in an instant: a common hazard of the "roast," when the speaker crosses the line between a friendly jibe and an unfriendly barb toward the honoree. The mood of the event changes instantly to one of unease and angst. A celebration needs a clean agenda infused with a spirit of genuine good will.

Then there is the institutional or civic celebration: the company party, club festivity, charity dinner or ball, political fundraiser. It recognizes a special community: the company, the club, the civic group, the supporters of a cause, the political party or candidate. It may have business or promotion or fund-raising as a goal, or just networking for its own sake. Often it is essentially social: an occasion for people to mingle and expand their acquaintance and enjoy each other's company and share ideas and experiences, or just see and be seen. The unstated social price of admission is to participate fully in the event: dress up, make an effort, be bright and smart and engaging and congenial.

And then, the calendar holidays: commemorative days (the Fourth of July, Bastille Day; Presidents Day; Martin Luther King Day); cultural holidays (Mardi Gras, "River Fire" in Providence, RI, "First Night" celebrations of the arts); institutional holidays (Labor Day, Bank Holidays in Britain, United Nations Day);

seasonal or environmental holidays (Thanksgiving, the Winter Solstice, Earth Day); and the many religious holidays. Here we remember and celebrate our antecedents, our history, our culture, our land and our religion. The processions and speeches remind us that we are part of a historical and cultural continuum, that we cannot forget or take for granted the great achievements, efforts and sacrifices of our benefactors of the past and present. (Too often, the commemorative days are subverted into blatantly commercial or recreational opportunities: Buy a car! Go to the beach!) Holidays also are a chance to slow down and just enjoy the natural and the human-made world—to relish our access to its beauty and bounty and diversions. We put our troubles on hold—enjoy the moment.

Town and village life is energized by the social center of the market or the bazaar (or the mall), where we congregate to sell and buy and celebrate the produce and products of our trade, and to enjoy the diverse company and hubbub. All regions host and take pride in their town and country fairs, their flea markets, their weekly farmer's markets, their crafts shows.

In the normal course of the day, throughout the world, in village or town or city, people gather together. After school, the young flock to the mall. In the evening, a swarm of families and friends, dressed to be seen, flow in a ritual *passeggiata* down an old city boulevard or around a public square. At the shore, before or after dinner, strollers converge on the boardwalk or along the beach. In rural countryside, families meet at a home, a local hall or a pub for a *ceilidh*—music and dancing, food and chatter—or for an ice cream social, or a bingo night. The get-togethers fulfill the natural need to stay in touch, enjoy each other's company, share news and information and stories and plans. At the base camp of society, the family, the at-home meal remains the nexus of family life, today as always. Around the table, at the counter, in front of the TV with pizza, we renew connections with each other, vital to our sense of well-being and our need to be part of a group.

The need for society and for autonomy—reliance on others and independence—compete within us, and we do our best to strike the balance which meets our own need. There is an irony here: to be effective and comfortable in the group, we need a healthy sense of our own autonomy; yet we rely on the support of the group, to work comfortably and effectively alone.

Honors, Awards and Prizes

Another "acknowledgment and celebration" is the practice of conferring honors, awards and prizes for special achievement. As a society, we admire and recognize individuals or groups who make an out-of-the-ordinary contribution to the community, or who attain special distinction in some area. We single them out. We award the Pulitzer Prize for brilliant scholarship and writing; we select Nobel laureates who have advanced the cause of peace; we root for our favorite stars and films at the Academy Awards; we warm with pride in our town's newest Eagle Scout; we put on a big parade for our winning team. The honorees become celebrities, for a least one shining moment. We appreciate what they have done to "make the world a better place;" we take inspiration from their example. The awards and honors remind us that exceptional work *can* bring prizes and recognition: sometimes there *is* a gold medal; an embossed-and-blue-ribboned citation with a long recitation of "Whereas's," signed with a flourish by the mayor; a gleaming trophy; or a welcome check.

Reflect, enjoy, celebrate. Have fun and give thanks. In a secular life, in which we do not look Above or After for comfort, hope and joy, we relish instead our ordinary and extraordinary pleasures. They are not indulgences, but a vital part of who we are. We have all of life to live—to learn and teach, to act, to do good—and all of existence to enjoy and celebrate.

※ ※ ※

The Manual: In Conclusion

If we believe in "the job" of a secular life—in this case, to learn and teach, to act, to do good, to have fun (and to celebrate)—naturally we want to carry out the job as best we can every day, and also incorporate "what works" into broader policies for our society. As individuals in an enormous and diverse human community, we are arrayed across a wide spectrum of abilities and aspirations, each of us choosing our particular role. Presumably, society functions well if the whole array is in some semblance of balance—and if we remember, often enough, to "feed the good wolf."

Life is rich, and the tapestry of the world a matchlessly amazing ever-changing backdrop to our hard times and good times, our work and our play. So we reflect on it, relish it, mine it for its gold. And give thanks accordingly.

Our plate is full. The cosmos is enough.

※ ※ ※

End Notes

Introduction
[1] Neuhaus writes of "'the naked public square,' meaning public life stripped of religious practice and conviction." Richard John Neuhaus, "Faith and Reason," *Boston Sunday Globe*, 12/24/06, p. C4.

Chapter 1
[2] Even then, in an age steeped in religious tradition, in which he was the seventh in a family line of Christian ministers, Emerson arrived early at the personal conviction that religion is "to do right. It is to love, it is to serve, it is to think, it is to be humble." A traumatic personal loss, the death of his adored young wife, had thrown him into a hard period of soul-searching, culminating in his new view.

"Religion in the mind is not credulity, and in the practice is not form. It is a life. It is the order and soundness of a man. It is not something else *to be got,* to be added, but is a new life of those faculties you have."

His biographer Ralph Rusk concludes, "He was simply grinding religion down to morals, as he now habitually did." (Ralph L. Rusk, *The Life of Ralph Waldo Emerson*, New York: Charles Scribner's Sons, 1949, pp. 161-162. Rusk citation: J, II, 492. MS CCE to WmE(b), 6 July 1832.)

[3] Megan Marshall, *ThePeabody Sisters*, Boston: Mariner, Houghton Mifflin Company, 2006, p. 2.

[4] Winnie Hu, "In a New Generation of College Students, Many Opt for the Life Examined," Education Section, *The New York Times*, April 6, 2008.

[5] The contemporary "academy" of philosophy, in the tradition of its antecedents and building on their work, continues to study and speculate about existence, human consciousness, morality and meaning. Today's elite thinkers—the late political philosopher John Rawls for example, or the moral philosophers Christine Korsgaard and Peter Singer—take on the intellectual burden of explaining us to ourselves in contemporary times, especially our moral selves, and the opaque puzzle of human consciousness itself. (What is consciousness? How did morality evolve?) The modern ranks are swelled by able and enthusiastic younger thinkers such as Professor Sean Dorrance Kelly, touted as "the first philosopher since the celebrated William James (1842-1910) to have a laboratory at Harvard," for his experiments on "very tiny problems" of psychophysics. Kelly wonders if, drawing on the lessons of Homer's Greece, we may recapture "the beginnings of the notion of the sacred in modern life.... In this way, one can hope to re-enchant the world." (Kelly came to philosophy by way of mathematics, computer science, neuroscience and even amateur robotics.) But the new and old academic philosophy is densely referential (sometimes in

danger of being a closed loop?). The discussion is apt to be so convoluted, so wound up in the technical terminology of philosophy, anthropology, psychology, mathematics and other disciplines, as to be practically inaccessible to most of us. Meanwhile, the different areas of philosophical study are becoming so intermingled—and at the same time so specialized—that it is ever more challenging to keep tabs on them. We can think of this trend as a good thing. The late philosopher Richard Rorty, a notorious but well-liked provocateur in his own profession (who reveled in questioning the relevance of philosophy), objected to attempts to make philosophy into an "autonomous quasiscience."

"The more philosophy interacts with other human activities—not just natural science, but art, literature, religion and politics as well—the more relevant to cultural politics it becomes, and thus the more useful."

In April 2007, Jonah Lehrer of the *Boston Sunday Globe*, in a piece called "Hearts and Minds," reported on a symposium celebrating the "cognitive revolution," where linguist Noam Chomsky and other field-leading psychologists and neuroscientists have been studying scientifically the actual processes of thought, fueling "a generation of productive research, yielding deep insights into many aspects of thought, including memory, language and perception." Upending the old-school distinction between *thought* and *feeling* –between the intellect and the emotions—the experts now conclude that "it is impossible to understand how we think without understanding how we feel."

Chapter 2
[6] Poem "Anyway," reportedly hung by Mother Teresa at her Calcutta orphanage
[7] Robert L. Humphrey, J.D., *Values for a New Millennium* (Life Values Press, 2005), p.51.)
This statement is the basis of a values system propounded by Robert L Humphrey, J.D., a Marine Corps veteran of the battle of Iwo Jima in World War II, and a lifelong State Department consultant and innovator in combating Ugly American syndrome in the U.S. military overseas. Humphrey, a national class boxer, Marine, graduate of Harvard Law School and the Fletcher School of Law and Diplomacy, devoted his life to discovering and teaching a values system based on what he believed to be a "natural law" of humankind, represented by the statement quoted above. In his book *Values for a New Millennium* (published in 1992 and republished in 2005), he remarks,

"1. You can get yourself into the second-most dangerous position anywhere in the world by threatening a person's life.
2. If that is second, what is the most dangerous action?..[T]hreatening someone's loved ones.
That describes the most basic nature of the human animal."
(Robert L Humphrey, *Values for a New Millennium* (The Life Values Press, 2005), p. 148)

Chapter 3
[8] Editor in Chief, Philip Babcock Gove, Ph.D., *Webster's Third New International Dictionary of the English Language, Unabridged* (Springfield, MA: G. & C. Merriam Company, 1965), p. 2198.
[9] Peter Sarstedt song, "Where do you go to my Lovely," 1969
[10] See Daniel C. Dennett, "Beliefs designed to be professed," *Breaking the Spell*, New York: Viking, 2006, pp. 226-229.
[11] The contemporary French philosopher Michel Onfray , an anti-theist and "modern" hedonist, argues for a life devoted to pleasure (whatever that is) and personal freedom, but tempered by reason.
[12] The Jamaican cultural observer Orlando Patterson, in a January 2007 column in *The New York Times*, delivers a sobering update on "The Other Losing War."

> "Preoccupation with Iraq has drawn attention from another unwinnable American war that has been far more destructive of life both at home and abroad and has caused far greater collateral damage in other countries, in addition to spreading contempt for American foreign engagements. This is the failed war on drugs. ...
> ...Recent surveys indicate a steady increase in the use of illicit drugs: more than 40 percent of Americans have used them at some point. Nearly all Caribbean societies are involved with narcotrafficking.... In 2001, illicit drug shipments in the region were worth more money than the top five legitimate exports combined. The results have been devastating....
> ...[Jamaica's minister of national security says] drugs sustain a 'self-perpetuating culture of extreme violence.'"

(Orlando Patterson, "The Other Losing War," Guest Column, *The New York Times*, Jan. 13, 2007.)
Of course the drug-related problems of the Caribbean and the USA are just a part of a seemingly intractable globe-spanning plague of addiction and crime caused by cocaine, heroin, methamphetamines and their lethally addictive ilk.
[13] Brooke Allen, *Moral Minority: Our Skeptical Founding Fathers*, (Chicago: Ivan R. Dee, 2006) p.xiii.
[14] Brooke Allen, *Moral Minority*, p. xii-xiii.
[15] Daniel Goleman, *Social Intelligence* (New York: Bantam Books, 2006), p. 60.
[16] Daniel Goleman, *Social Intelligence*, p. 62.

Chapter 4
[17] "Ecevit buried amid secularist chants," Reuters, cn.com/2006/WORLD/europed/11/11/, 2006.
[18] Ryan J. Foley, Associated Press, "Group gathers in Wis., but not under God," *The Boston Globe*,

Oct. 12, 2007, p. A7.

[19] Pippa Norris and Ronald Inglehart, *Sacred and Secular* (Cambridge University Press, 2004), p.4. Norris and Inglehart conclude that the critique of the doubters "relies too heavily on selected anomalies and focuses too heavily on the United States (which happens to be a striking deviant case) rather than comparing systematic evidence across a broad range of rich and poor societies." (Ibid., p. 4)

[20] Norris and Inglehart's thesis, which they believe is supported by the evidence, is that the main factor in determining religiosity is "the extent to which people have a sense of existential security—that is the feeling that survival is secure enough that it can be taken for granted," and that more security results in less religiosity. The implication of their finding for American society—high on affluence but with significant inequality—is that to achieve stability and "existential security" the USA must take exceptional measures to advance equality, to reduce the "expectation gap" of those on the low end. And that the same mission must be addressed globally, in order to advance global stability. (*Sacred and Secular,* p.4.)

[21] Norris and Inglehart, *Sacred and Secular,* pp. 24, 25.

[22] Norris and Inglehart, *Sacred and Secular,* "Table 3.1 Religiosity by Type of Society."

[23] U.S. Census (USC), International DataBase (IDB), "Countries Ranked by Population: 2006." [Website on file]

[24] Norris and Inglehart, *Sacred and Secular,* Table 3.1.

[25] European Values Study Group and World Values Survey Association ["WVS"],"9062000.-Values Surveys: F034.-Religious Person, United States," *The Values Surveys 1981-2004.*

[26] "F001.-Thinking about meaning and purpose of life: China 2001," WVS.

[27] Norris and Inglehart, *Sacred and Secular,* p. 240.

[28] "F034.-Religious person: India 2001," WVS.

[29] Norris and Inglehart, *Sacred and Secular,* p. 25.

[30] Norris and Inglehart, *Sacred and Secular,* p. 92.

[31] Norris and Inglehart, *Sacred and Secular,* p. 92.

[32] Norris and Inglehart, *Sacred and Secular,* p. 93.

[33] Norris and Inglehart, *Sacred and Secular,* p. 94.

[34] Norris and Inglehart, *Sacred and Secular* , p. 105.

[35] Norris and Inglehart, *Sacred and Secular,* p. 75.

[36] Norris and Inglehart, *Sacred and Secular,* p. 78.

[37] Laurie Goodstein, "Evangelicals Fear the Loss of Their Teenagers," *The New York Times,* Oct. 6, 2006.

[38] Norris and Inglehart, *Sacred and Secular,* p. 91.

[39] Norris and Inglehart, *Sacred and Secular,* p. 91.

[40] Norris and Inglehart, *Sacred and Secular* , p. 92.

[41] Leon Wieseltier, "The God Genome," Book Review, *New York Times,* Feb. 19, 2006.
[42] George Johnson, "A Free-for-All on Science and Religion," *New York Times,* Nov. 21, 2006.

Chapter 5
[43] The John Templeton Foundation, www.templeton.org.belief, May 2008.
[44] In fairness to his views, it is noted that Richardson also argued, on the converse, that there is something "pedestrian, limiting, bald in choosing to living exclusively in a world of matter, of the concrete, ... the actual." Certainly not a Be-ist view of reality. (Robert D. Richardson, "Emerson and the Perennial Philosophy," May 25, 2003.)
42 Marc D. Hauser, *Moral Minds* (New York: HarperCollins Publishers, 2006), Part II, Ch. 7, "What is 'Good'?"

Chapter 6
[46] The evolutionary biologist Elisabet Sahtouris writes about the fundamental role of co-operation in the survival and sustainable success of species. She argues that nature provides practical and effective examples of cooperation that could be used to improve the relations of human society—business, government, international relations—and help humanity evolve more harmoniously in its environment.

" 'Earth is alive,' Sahtouris explains.

> 'It is not a mechanical, hierarchical system, but an organic, self-organizing system. The whole universe is a living enterprise that organizes itself. It's *autopoietic,* a definition of living entities as constantly creating themselves and their parts from within in relation to their environment. All healthy, living systems self-organize and maintain themselves by the same principles, whether as a single cell, your body, an ecosystem or a global human culture.' "

(Tijn Touber , *Ode,* July/August 2006, p. 56-57.)

[47] A synthesizing thinker about global power, Nye conceives of power as a complex three-dimensional chess game:

> "On the top chessboard, military power is largely unipolar [i.e.held by the USA].... But on the middle chessboard, economic power is multi-polar [USA, Europe, Japan, China].... The bottom chessboard is the realm of transnational relations that cross borders outside government control, and has widely dispersed power [and connectivity: electronic banking, the internet, NGOs, educational and scientific institutions, health and medical issues, climate change, the arts and humanities, terrorist networks]... [W]hen you are in a three-dimensional game, you will lose if you focus only on the interstate military board and fail to notice the other boards and the vertical connections among them."

(Joseph S. Nye, Jr., *The Paradox of American Power: Why the World's Only Superpower Can't Go It Alone* (Oxford University Press, 2002), p.39.)

[48] The late supply-side economist Jude Wanniski published a broad-sweeping, succinct, and readable synthesis of economics in 1978, *The Way the World Works: How Economies Fail—and Succeed*. Counter to the prevailing wisdom, he makes a historical case that lower and fairer taxes foster savings and production; but his other powerful concept is in the economics of international development, where he argues for the export of "intellectual capital," rather than hard aid such as hydroelectric dams and highways.

[49] The Peruvian economist Hernando DeSoto, looking globally at the "informal" sector in developing countries, presents a strong new case for reforming private property rights to pave the way for capital formation and economic success. His ideas have become popularized with his bestselling book, *The Mystery of Capital: Why Capitalism Triumphs in the West and Fails Everywhere*, published in 2000.

[50] The cognitive psychologist Elizabeth Spelke runs a research project on the "innate" knowledge babies are born with, the core knowledge that they use to make sense of experience. Yet Spelke has a wider impact as a result of her philosophical approach to the study of human differences, where she focuses on *commonality*, rather than distinctions, as between males and females. (Margaret Talbot, "The Baby Lab: How Elizabeth Spelke peers into the infant mind," *The New Yorker*, Sep. 4, 2006, pp. 91-101.)

[51] Robert Fulford of the Canadian *National Post* describes Denis Dutton's online magazine—whose motto "Veritas odit moras" means "Truth hates delay"—as "an aggregator...but much more than that. It's both a daily reminder of the riches available in the publications of the world and a map to finding those riches....Apparently not a sparrow falls, intellectually speaking, without [the editors'] knowledge." In Fulford's estimation,

> "A & LD does for ideas what the Bloomberg service does for commerce. It watches developments, sorts things out, tells you what you need to know. Over time its ability to make connections may turn out to be even more important than the stock market."

(Robert Fulford, "A buffet sure to leave you hungry," *National Post*, CanWest Interactive, 2007, canada.com network.)

[52] Harvey Blume, "Q&A: John Searle," "Ideas" Section, *Boston Globe*, Feb. 4, 2007, p. E3.

[53] Kevin Kelly, *Out of Control* (Reading, MA: Addison-Wesley, 1995 ed.), pp. 471-472.

[54] Brian Greene, *The Fabric of the Cosmos* (New York: Vintage Books, 2005), p. 5.

[55] Cornelia Dean, "She Calls It 'Phenomena.' Everyone Else Calls It Art," *The New York Times*, Jun. 12, 2007.

[56] Jonathan Gottschall, "Measure for Measure," Ideas, *Boston Sunday Globe*, May 11, 2008, p. D1-2.

[57] Bella English, "How do I build thee? Let me count the ways," *Boston Globe*, Dec. 30, 2006, p. D1.

[58] Nicholas D. Kristof, "Do-Gooders with Spreadsheets," *New York Times*, Op-Ed, Jan. 30, 2006.

[59] Roger Cohen, "'The American' in France," Op-Ed, *The New York Times*, Oct. 18. 2007.

[60] Of course, some also will risk their lives for cash-plus-the-thrill-of-danger (mercenaries); or from coercion (child soldiers), or messianic fervor (suicide bombers), or from a combination of motives: financial incentive, an appetite for risk, plus serving "the good" (law enforcers, firefighters, rescue squads, and military forces). And some will put their lives at considerable risk to accomplish a personal challenge: climbing Mt. Everest, flying an experimental airplane, a single-hand voyage across the Southern Oceans.

[61] From the papers of Capt. William ("Bing") Emerson, USMC, killed in action in Vietnam,
November 20, 1968.

Chapter 7

[62] We tout Honesty as one of our basic principles, but how do we do? A problem through the ages, and one that continues to trouble us today. In September 2006 the Josephson Institute of Ethics, a nonprofit organization that conducts training in business ethics and character education, released results of a survey of 36,122 U.S. high school students:

- 61% have cheated on an exam in the past year.
- 28% have stolen from a store.
- 23% have stolen from a parent or relative.
- 39% have lied to save money.

(Lyric Wallwork Winik, "Cheating Nation," Intelligence Report, *Parade*, Oct. 15, 2006.)

[63] Alan M. MacRobert, "See the light in winter's darkness," Star Watch, *Boston Globe*, Jan. 6, 2007.

Chapter 8

[64] Shaila Dewan, "In Setback for New Orleans, Fed-Up Residents Give Up," *The New York Times*, Feb. 16, 2007.

[65] Donald G. McNeil, Jr., "Child Mortality at Record Low; Further Drop Seen," *The New York Times*, Sep. 13, 2007.

[66] Professor Grindle went on to explain that the honeymoon of the "third wave of democracy" is over—that the world need new forms of democracy to suit nations breaking away from a long history of authoritarian rule and a deep divide between the rich and the poor. She stressed the need for *economic* as well as political democracy; strong institutions for social and economic order and

justice; education, especially for girls and women; and better strategies to combat AIDS and drug addiction.
(Kennedy School of Government Dean's Conference, Harvard University, May 12-14, 2005.)

[67] "World Population Prospects: The 2006 Revision," Population Division, United Nations, 2007.

[68] Neil Howe and William Strauss, *Millennials Rising: The Next Great Generation* (Vintage Books, 2000), and *Millennials Go to College* (American Association of Collegiate Registrars and Admissions Officers, 2003).

[69] David Brooks, "Children of Polarization," Op-Ed, *The New York Times*, Feb. 4, 2007.

[70] Linda K. Wertheimer, "Join the club: Colleges see surge in new student groups," *The Boston Globe*, Oct. 27, 2007, p. A1.

[71] John J. Reilly, Review of *Millennials Rising: The Next Great Generation*, www.johnreilly.info.miri.htm.

[72] Peter Wehner and Yuval Levin, "Crime, Drugs, Welfare—and Other Good News," *Commentary*, Dec. 2007.

[73] "World Question Center,"2007, "What are you optimistic about?" *Edge*,edge.org/q2007/q07_I.html.

[74] Special Report: Sudan, "Glittering towers in a war zone," *The Economist*, Sep. 9, 2006, p. 27.

[75] Stephen Jay Gould, "In Praise of Charles Darwin," *Discover* (TimeMagazine, 1982), reprinted as Foreword; Benjamin Farrington, *What Darwin Really Said* (New York: Shocken Books, 1966, 1982),p. xv.

[76] Adam Gopnik, "Rewriting Nature: Charles Darwin, natural novelist," *The New Yorker*, Oct. 23, 2006, p. 59.

[77] In 1976 the novelist James Carroll, on a book tour touting his first novel, *Madonna Red,* spoke about the Jesuit concept that we seek absolute answers through faith, we are "Pilgrims of the Absolute."

[78] The cover story in *Popular Mechanics* in December 2006: "Killer Asteroid: It's Coming Our Way." Subsequently it has been determined that the likelihood of "Apophis," an 820-foot-wide 25-million-ton "pockmarked rock," hitting the Earth at 28,000 m.p.h. on Friday, April 13th, 2029, is significantly less than the 0.03% risk cited in the article. But Apophis is only one of more than 100,000 known "rocks" that hurtle past the home planet.
(David Noland, "the threat is out there," *Popular Mechanics,* Vol. 183, No. 12, Dec. 2006, p. 83.)

Chapter 9

[79] Ralph Waldo Emerson, "Country Life"

[80] Verlyn Klinkenborg, "Appreciations: Ryzard Kapuscinski," Op Ed, *New York Times,* Feb. 2, 2007.

[81] "Positive prejudice: Really loving your neighbour," *The Economist*, 3/17/07, p. 66. Also, see Todd L. Pittinsky, S. A. Rosenthal and R.M. Montoya, "Moving Beyond Tolerance: Allophilia Theory and Measurement," presented to the Society for Personality and Social Psychology, Jan. 2007.

[82] In this context, would it be fitting to retitle the well-known UN document, the "Universal Declaration of Human *Needs and Aspirations*"? For it is only *legal and civil action*, by individual governments and communities who exercise authority, which can convert the long list of needs and aspirations to "rights." Each time that happens, it is an individual and communal triumph for that particular government and its people, and can be honored and recognized as such. And even then, only vigilant follow-up—such as funding and the creation of required programs and general acceptance of the new law and custom—can assure that the "right" will be upheld for the citizens on whom it is conferred.

[83] John Schaeffer, "Relocalize Now!" *Real Goods*, Resource Guide, Spring 2007, p. 2.

[84] Ralph Waldo Emerson, "Sunrise," *Collected Poems and Translations of Ralph Waldo Emerson*, Eds. Harold Bloom, Paul Kane (Library of America, 1994), p. 395, note pp. 612-613.

Chapter 10

[85] After a 2.88-billion-mile round trip to the other side of Mars' orbit, NASA's robot spacecraft Stardust returned to Earth in January 2006 with thousands of tiny particles from the 4.5 billion-year-old comet Wild 2.

> "Comet dust seems to be a real zoo of things... all indicate that when the solar system was forming there was a whole lot of mixing going on.... It's not just dust and particles," said Scott Sandford of NASA. "We are working on rocks... We want to know how these rocks were formed and how they became parts of comets that were formed out on the edge of the solar system."

(Warren E. Leary, "Researchers Find Surprise in Makeup of a Comet," *New York Times*, 12/15/06.)

[86] David Chanoff, "Education Is My Mother and My Father," *The American Scholar*, Vol. 74, No. 4, Autumn 2005.

[87] Ibid, p. 45.

[88] Natalie Angier, "In Science Classrooms, a Blast of Fresh O_2," Basics, *The New York Times*, Oct. 30, 2007.)

Chapter 11

[89] Sandra Aamodt and Sam Wang, "Exercise on the Brain," Op-Ed, *The New York Times*, Nov. 8, 2007.

[90] Drake Bennett, "Don't Just Stand There, THINK," "Ideas," *The Boston Globe*, Jan. 13, 2008, p. 1-2.

[91] *Harvard Women's Health Watch*, Oct. 2005, p. 4.

Chapter 12

[92] Martin E.G. Seligman, Letter, "The Mail," *The New Yorker,* Mar. 20, 2006, p.20.

[93] John Lanchester, "Pursuing Happiness," *The New Yorker,* Feb. 27, 2006, p. 81.

[94] Craig Lambert, "The Science of Happiness," *Harvard Magazine,* p. 26, Jan-Feb 2007.

[95] "Economics discovers its feelings," *The Economist,* Dec. 23, 2006, p. 35.

[96] "Daniel Gilbert's 'Stumbling on Happiness' lands top book prize." *Harvard University Gazette,* May 17-23, 2007, p. 8.

[97] The researcher spoke on Christopher Lydon's WBUR radio show "The Connection" in the late 1990s.

[98] Barry Schwartz, "Money for Nothing," Op-Ed, *New York Times,* July 2, 2007.

[99] Christopher and Miranda Meyer, The Mail, *The New Yorker,* July 30, 2007, p. 8.

[100] Catherine Drinker Bowen, *Yankee from Olympus: Justice Holmes and His Family* (Boston: Little, Brown and Company, 1944), p. 225.

[101] John Tierney, Findings, "Taxes a Pleasure? Check the Brain Scan." *New York Times,* June 19, 2007.

[102] Jonathan Weiner, "Darwin at the Zoo," Review, *Scientific American,* Dec. 2006, pp. 114, 116.

[103] Franz de Waal, *Primates and Philosophers: How Morality Evolved* (Princeton: Princeton University Press, 2006)

[104] Marc Hauser, *Moral Minds,* p. xviii.

[105] Marc Hauser, *Moral Minds,* p. 36.

[106] Marc Hauser, *Moral Minds,* p. 60.

[107] The "impartial observer" as neutral arbiter is an old concept, of course. Frans de Waal and his colleagues, in their discussion of *disinterestedness* —as well as universality —as requirements of morality, often refer to Adam Smith's "impartial spectator" (1759) who must decide right from wrong. (Frans de Waal, *Primates and Philosophers,* p. 20; Philip Kitcher, *Primates and Philosophers,* p. 133; Adam Smith, *A Theory of Moral Sentiment* (New York: Modern Library, 1937 [1759]).

[108] Dinitia Smith, "A Writer Looks to Her History and Reaps an Award," *New York Times,* Oct. 26, 2006, p. B3.

[109] Bob Herbert, "An American Obsession," Op Ed, *New York Times,* Feb. 2, 2006.

[110] Maggie Jackson, "Repeat after me: 'Welcome home, dear,'" Balancing Acts, *The Boston Globe,* Feb. 12, 2006, pp. G1, G7.

[111] Roland Fryer, *Tradeoffs for Different Types of Well-Being: An Economic Approach to Cultural Capital:* Abstract, Harvard University, June 3003.
[112] Richard Stengel, "A Time To Serve," *Time*, Sep. 10, 2007, pp. 49-67.
[113] Caroline Kennedy, "Making a Difference at Home," *Time*, Sep. 10, 2007, p. 68.
[114] Malcolm Gladwell, *The Tipping Point* (New York: Little, Brown and Company, 2002) p. 140.
[115] Malcolm Gladwell, *The Tipping Point*, p. 146.
[116] Malcolm Gladwell, *The Tipping Point*, p. 167.
[117] Robert Campbell, "Why we like the buildings we like," *Boston Sunday Globe*, Jan. 14, 2007, p. N4.
[118] On social entrepreneurship, see *How to Change the World: Social Entrepreneurs and the Power of New Ideas* by David Borstein (Oxford University Press, 2004). On social psychology, see *Social Intelligence: The New Science of Human Relationships* by Daniel Goleman (Bantam Books, 2006).
[119] "Wilson shares insights on evolution," *Inside Binghamton University*, Vol. 28, No. 17, Jan. 25, 2007.
[120] Alvin Powell, "Summers, Lehrer urge change," *Harvard University Gazette*, June 15, 2006, pp. 9-10.
[121] Ronald Inglehart, Graph: "Authority and Value Systems," *Modernization and Postmodernization* (Princeton, 1997).

Chapter 13

[122] A short reading list:
Edward O. Wilson, *The Diversity of Life* (New York: W.W. Norton & Company, 1992); and *Consilience: The Unity of Knowledge* (New York: Alfred A. Knopf, 1998);
Jared Diamond, *Guns, Germs and Steel: The Fates of Human Societies* (New York: W.W. Norton & Company, 1999);
Brian Greene, *The Fabric of the Cosmos: Space, Time and the Texture of Reality* (New York: Random House, Inc., 2004);
Daniel Goleman, *Emotional Intelligence* (New York: Bantam Dell, 1995, 2005), *Social Intelligence* (New York: Bantam Dell, 2006).
[123] Kevin Kelly, Out of Control: The New Biology of Machines, Social Systems, and the Economic World (Reading, MA: Addison-Wesley, 1994), p. 471.
[124] See Joseph S. Nye, Jr., *Soft Power: The Means to Success in World Politics* (New York: Public Affairs, 2004)

Chapter 14

[125] Ruth Walker, "Fresh Faces in the Humanities: Alison Frank," *Harvard University Offices of News & Public Affairs,* (Harvard University, 2007), Apr. 13, 2006, p. 12.

[126] David Servan-Schreiber, *The Instinct to Heal* (Rodale, 2003).

[127] Katherine Stirling, "Va Bene," *The New Yorker*, Apr. 7, 2008, p. 27.

[128] The *New York Times* columnist Paul Krugman, remembering Molly Ivins, makes the point that Ivins' "marks" were the powerful, that she was a champion of the truth and fairness in her satire. He quotes her, in a *Mother Jones* piece attacking the conservative Rush Limbaugh: "Satire... has historically been the weapon of powerless people aimed at the powerful. When you use satire against powerless people ... it is like kicking a cripple." (Paul Krugman, "Missing Molly Ivins," Op-Ed, *New York Times*, Feb. 2, 2007.)

[129] Daniel Goleman, *Social Intelligence*, p. 178.

[130] Ariel Levy, *Female Chauvinist Pigs: Women and the Rise of Raunch Culture* (New York: Free Press, Simon Schuster, Inc., 2005), p. 33.

[131] Edna St. Vincent Millay, untitled sonnet [add correct citation]

[132] John Rockwell, "Crossing Over a Thin Line From Sacred to Secular," Dance Review, *New York Times*, Dec. 7, 2006.

[133] Lauren Collins, "Foreign Exchange: Say Cheese!" *The New Yorker*, Jan. 22, 2007, p. 31.

[134] Ralph Waldo Emerson, untitled draft poem, eds. Harold Bloom and Paul Kane, *Collected Poems and Translations of Ralph Waldo Emerson*(Library of America, 1994), p.422.

[135] David Brooks, "A Partnership of Minds," Op-Ed, *The New York Times*, July 20,2007.

[136] Michael Shermer, "Skeptic: Bowling for God," *Scientific American*, Dec. 2006, p. 44.

[137] Michael Shermer, ibid.

[138] Neil Howe & William Strauss, *Millenials Go to College* (American Association of Collegiate Registrars and Admission Officers/LifeCourse Associates, 2003)

Bibliography

Book References

Allen, Brooke. *Moral Minority.* Chicago: Ivan R. Dee, 2006.

Bornstein, David. *How to Change the World.* Oxford: Oxford University Press, 2004.

Bowen, Catherine D. *Yankee from Olympus: Justice Holmes and His Family.* Boston: Little, Brown, 1944.

Chanoff, David. "Education Is My Mother and My Father," *The American Scholar,* Vol. 74, No. 4, Autumn 2005.

Dawkins, Richard. *The God Delusion,* Boston and New York: Houghton Mifflin, 2006.

Dennett, Daniel C. *Breaking the Spell.* New York: Viking Penguin, 2006.

Diamond, Jared. *Guns, Germs, and Steel.* New York: W. W. Norton, 1999, 1997.

Desai, Kiran. *The Inheritance of Loss.* New York: Grove Press, 2006.

DeSoto, Hernando. *The Mystery of Capital: Why Capitalism Triumphs in the West and Fails Everywhere Else.* London: Bantam, 2000.

De Waal, Franz. *Primates and Philosophers: How Morality Evolved.* Princeton: Princeton University Press, 2006.

Emerson, Edward W. *Emerson in Concord.* Boston and New York: Houghton Mifflin, 1888, 1916.

Emerson, Ralph Waldo. *The Selected Writings of Ralph Waldo Emerson.* Brooks Atkinson, Ed. New York: The Modern Library, 1940, 1950.

Farrington, Benjamin. *What Darwin Really Said.* New York: Schocken Books, 1966, 1982.

Gladwell, Malcolm. *The Tipping Point.* New York and Boston: Little, Brown, 2000, 2002.

Goleman, Daniel. *Emotional Intelligence.* New York: Bantam Books, 1995, 2005.

---------. *Social Intelligence.* New York: Bantam Books, 2006.

Greene, Brian. *The Fabric of the Cosmos.* New York: Vintage Books, 2004, 2005.

Harris, Sam. *The End of Faith.* New York: W. W. Norton, 2004, 2005.

Hauser, Marc D. *Moral Minds,.* New York: HarperCollins, 2006.

Howe, Neil and William Strauss. *Millennials Go to College.* American Association of Collegiate Registrars and Admissions Officers, 2003.
----------. *Millennials Rising.* New York: Knopf, 2000.
Humphrey, Robert L. *Values for a New Millennium.* Spring Lake, NJ: The Life Values Press,1992, 2005.
Kelly, Kevin. *Out of Control: The New Biology of Machines, Social Systems, and the Economic World,* Reading, MA: Addison-Wesley, 1994.
Levy, Ariel. *Female Chauvinist Pigs: Women and the Rise of Raunch Culture.* New York: Free Press, 2005.
Menand, Louis. *The Metaphysical Club.* New York: Farrar, Straus and Giroux, 2001.
Marshall, Megan. *The Peabody Sisters.* Boston and New York: Houghton Mifflin, 2005, 2006.
Norris, Pippa and Ronald Inglehart. *Sacred and Secular: Religion and Politics Worldwide.* Cambridge: Cambridge University Press, 2004.
Nye, Joseph S., Jr. *The Paradox of American Power.* Oxford: Oxford University Press, 2002.
---------. *Soft Power.* New York: Public Affairs, 2004.
Rusk, Ralph L. *The Life of Ralph Waldo Emerson.* New York: Charles Scribner's Sons, 1949.
Servan-Schreiber, David. *The Instinct to Heal.* Rodale, 2003, 2004.
Wanniski, Jude. *The Way the World Works: How Economies Fail—and Succeed.* New York: Basic Books, 1978.
Wilson, Edward O. *Consilience: The Unity of Knowledge.* New York: Alfred A. Knopt, 1998.
---------. *The Diversity of Life.* New York: W. W. Norton, 1992.

Special Bibliographic Acknowledgment
The *World Values Survey* and the *European Values Survey* serve as primary data sources in Chapter 4, "Secularity Rising." The required citation for this valuable information source is as follows:
European Values Study Group and World Values Survey Association.
EUROPEAN AND WORLD VALUES SURVEYS FOUR-WAVE INTEGRATED DATA FILE, 1981-2004, v.20060423, 2006.
Aggregate File Producers: Analisis Sociologicos Econonomicas y Politicos (ASEP) and JD Systems (JDS), Madrid, Spain/Tilburg University,

The Netherlands. Data Files Suppliers: Analisis Sociologicos Economicos y Politicos (ASEP) and JD Systems (JDS), Madrid, Spain/Tilburg University, Tilburg, The Netherlands/ Zentralarchiv fur Empirische Sozialforschung (ZA), Cologne, Germany. Aggregate File Distributors: Analisis Sociologicos Economicos y Politicos (ASEP) and JD Systems (JDS), Madrid, Spain/Tilburg University, Tilburg, The Netherlands/Zentralarchiv fur Empirische Sozialforschung (ZA) Cologne, Germany.

Newspapers, Magazines and Other Sources
Refer to Endnotes for bibliographic information on these sources.

Acknowledgments

My four daughters (from near and afar) and patient husband stood by with encouragement and support for the duration of this, my first, book project. Thank you, Lize, Bec, Katrin, Susannah and Nick.

A special nod, too, to my kinsman, Mike Delaney, for his loyalty and interest, not to mention the dependable stream of erudite jibes and provocative e-links. May his own treatise prosper!

And my great thanks, also, to those who read all or parts of *The Be-ist* as it evolved, and were so generous and helpful with their insights, suggestions and enthusiasm: Cullen Murphy, Paul Elias and family, Anthony Dell, Claudia Thompson, Marnie Cochran, Bob Richardson, Wes Mott, Maja Stodte, Merloyd Lawrence, Ellen Emerson, Bruce Kohler and Lauran Emerson.

Made in the USA
Lexington, KY
07 February 2011